MY LIFE IS BASEBALL

MY LIFE IS BASEBALL

By Frank Robinson

With Al Silverman

Doubleday & Company, Inc.

Garden City, New York, 1968

For my wife Barbara, Frank Kevin, Nichelle, and
my mother, brothers, and sisters . . .
and to George Powles and everyone else who
helped me so much along the way

Contents

Contents

MY LIFE IS BASEBALL

1 *The Slide*

It is eleven-thirty in the morning when I stir in bed and decide I ought to get going. My wife, Barbara, has long since been up, getting Kevin off to day camp and Nichelle out in the yard, and now I am alone in the room and, outside, I can hear the voice of my little girl as she plays with her friends.

I ought to get going but I still feel tired. When I came home after the game I watched the Late Show, *Look in Any Window*, with Paul Anka. And if there was a Late Late Show I would have watched that, too. But there wasn't one and I finally crawled into bed about one-thirty.

And stayed awake a long time replaying the ball game.

We lost to the White Sox 5–4, lost in the ninth inning when they scored two runs. One of the few times this year we really battled, and still we lost. If we had won that game it would have given the team a real lift. I just got the feeling that if we won we might have beat 'em four straight. That might have set us on a winning streak.

And we need a winning streak bad. Now we're seven down in the loss column to the league-leading White Sox, and if we lose tonight it's eight down, and if we lose Wednesday it's nine down. And you can't bring those back.

And now we have to go out and beat the two best pitchers in the league, Joel Horlen first, then Gary Peters.

A four-game series with the White Sox and we have lost the first game. We must win the next three to get back in the race. Now the opportunity is ours. Now we don't have to look for help from anyone else. But there's not much time left for the World Champion Baltimore Orioles. It's late now, it's getting to the second half of the season. It's time to start putting something together.

Finally, I get dressed and Barbara immediately cheers me up. She has heard on the radio that I have been named to the American League All-Star team, that I received the second-highest amount of votes, second only to Al Kaline.

Is she satisfied? Not at all. "You better make the All-Star team next year," Barbara says. "Oh, I want so much to go to Houston."

I look at her. "I'm gonna be a manager next year."

"You," she snorts. "You can't manage your own child." She's right. When I try to scold Nichelle, who is two, the little one just stares at me and says, "Hey, man."

I eat dinner at two-thirty—ham, greens, sweet corn, salad, and a Coke—then I lie down and try to rest, try to make up for a restless night. I will be thirty-two years old on August 31 and I need my rest.

And at quarter to five I am ready to take off for the ball park. The kids are outside playing and I yell at them, "Okay, it's good-bye time. Come give me a kiss."

Kevin, who is five, comes up and kisses me nonchalantly. He is a free spirit, very cool. Then Nichelle takes her turn. "I love you," I whisper. "Love you," she says, which sounds a lot better to me than "Hey, man."

The trip to the ball park is twenty minutes and as soon as I park my car outside the gate I hear a boy holler at the top of his lungs, "Frank Robinson is coming!"

When I come through the gate the same boy says, as sweet as apple pie, "Hello, Mr. Robinson."

I say, "Thanks for the announcement."

I go in and sit down by my locker and someone comes by and ignores me and says to Paul Blair, who is stationed next to me, "Did Frank make the All-Star team?"

"No, not this year," Blair says, his mouth split in a wide, open grin.

I go along with it. "Heck," I say, "I can use the rest, the

time off." That sets Blair in motion. We call him "Motor-mouth" because he likes to ramble on and on and I finally shut him up by stealing behind him and wrapping a big white towel around his mouth.

I am sitting in my canvas chair in front of my cubicle, two purple rabbit's feet dangling from each end of the chair. Fans had sent them to me and they really help, if you're hitting.

I am dressing slowly, munching on a candy bar, when Jerry Hoffberger, the president of the ball club and a fine gentle-man, comes over. He has been overseas on a business trip and it is his first day back. He shakes hands with me and says, "I heard about you in Europe."

I say, "You don't believe that stuff, do you?"

He grins, but do I detect a slight strain in that grin?

He has heard about me all right. Not that I have been lead-ing the American League in hitting and runs batted in, and second in home runs. Not any of that, but what I had said in an interview after a losing game in Kansas City a week ago.

The Athletics had beaten us 9–2 that night and the loss put us one game under .500. I was disgusted and this Balti-more writer caught me just at the right time. "What do you think is really wrong with the ball club now?" he asked. "Why aren't we winning?"

I told him that I thought we just weren't playing real solid baseball, that we weren't playing up to our potential. We were too relaxed. We weren't taking the game to the op-position. I said, "The attitude seems to be, if we're winning it's okay, and if we're losing that's okay, too."

Then he asked me the jackpot question.

"Is there dissension in the club?"

I thought for a long time before answering him. Heck, when you're losing and you're supposed to be winning, people always figure it's because there's dissension in the ball club. I was trying to think of a word other than dissension, which wasn't the right word, anyway. Finally, I used another word, and I knew right away that wasn't the right word, either. Jealousy.

"What are they jealous of?" he asked.

I said, "They're jealous of me, I think."

I went back to the hotel and brooded all night over my choice of words, and the next day I wasn't disappointed. The story broke all over the country . . . and Europe, too, if Mr. Hoffberger wasn't just giving me the needle.

But I didn't mean jealousy. Sure, there are ballplayers who resent you, resent the money you're making, the fact that you won the Triple Crown and are still going good while maybe they're not going so good. That's only natural. Rather than jealousy, it was an over-all attitude. We were sitting back, expecting things to come up, waiting for the breaks. We weren't going out and forcing the breaks. When you're winning, you can do things a certain way. When you're losing, you can't do things the same way. You've got to change. You've got to do things different. So I won the Triple Crown in 1966. So I led the American League in batting, home runs, and runs batted in. The thing of it is, that was yesterday, and yesterday is over with.

Getting right down to it, I guess what I was trying to do was shake up the club, get them mad. If they got mad at me for saying what I thought, fine, maybe they'd go out and win a few games.

So far, though, we are still losing.

But now we have the chance to win, to close ground on the White Sox.

The first three innings are scoreless, Steve Barber pitching against Horlen. In the top of the fourth, a soft, sinking line drive is hit out to me and I go down on one knee to catch it but lose the ball in the lights; it hits off the heel of my glove and they give me an error, my first error in ninety-nine games. But the next batter, Tommie Agee, hits into the double play and we're out of it.

I am the first hitter in the last of the fourth and Horlen feeds me a curve ball and I remember hitting it deep to short, and remember it breaking through the shortstop for the base hit.

And that's all I remember until I wake up on the rubbing table in the trainer's room, my head throbbing, my memory clogged, feeling as strange as I have ever felt in my life.

Then, somehow, I am dressed and Joe Bride, our publicity man, is steering me to my car. He gets in the driver's seat and the next thing I know I am lying on a bed at Sinai Hospital and doctors and nurses are coming in and out all night long. And I am wondering what is happening, and why it is that I am here, still in my shorts, lying in a hospital bed in the emergency room of a busy hospital.

Later, they told me about it. I was on first base when Brooks Robinson hit a ground ball to third. Dick Kenworthy went to Al Weis at second base for the force, and I went into second to break up the double play. One Baltimore writer said I went in there like the Marines storming Inchon. I don't know. I expect I went in there the way I always go into second base. I feel it's good to bump a guy even if I know I'm out. To hit him, or nudge him, or let him know you're there, let him know you'll be doing that when the play is close. I think it's good baseball. It's going to make him think a little bit. He's going to say to himself, this guy hit me when he was out by five or six feet on an easy play. Here comes a close play. Where is he? Sometimes you get them to mess up the play or drop the ball or hurry the throw to first base and blow the double play. I think that's the only way to play this game and that's the only way I'm ever going to play it.

And that's the way I must have gone into second base, but maybe there was more this time. Maybe I was mad about that error in the top of the inning. Maybe I was mad about the losing ball game the night before. Maybe I was thinking to myself, this is the time to do something, this is the time to shake up this ball club, this is the time to get something going.

It must have been a hard slide judging by the results. Al Weis's knee apparently came up and made contact with my head, just over the left eye. When the dust cleared, there we both were, flat on our backs. I was lying on my side, two feet from the bag, unconscious. The umpire had called me safe; he said Weis had come off the bag too soon. But I couldn't get back to the bag. I was far, far away.

Our third-base coach, Billy Hunter, was out there and they said he looked like he wanted to pick me up and dump me on the bag. Ken Berry came all the way in from right field and hollered for the ball and they threw it to him and he made the tag on me. And I never felt it.

Weis got up and walked off the field, then was sent to the same hospital as me, then flown back to Chicago, for knee surgery.

I was out for about five minutes. Later they told me I had walked off the field under my own power, and this amazed me. I thought I had been carried off. But I wasn't too rational. Somebody asked me what day it was and I was supposed to have said, "a good day to play ball." They asked me what town I was in and I said something about California and UCLA. A brain concussion sometimes does funny things to you.

Barbara comes into the emergency room the first thing in the morning and she looks beautiful to me, both of her. I believe I am seeing double.

"What's the matter with you?" she says, wiping at her eyes.

"Did we win?" I ask.

"No, we lost, 5–0. What happened to you?"

"I don't remember anything," I say. "I remember the hit, that's all."

"I guess you know you're not playing ball tomorrow," she says.

"If I can see," I say.

"No, you're not. I'll throw a block on you."

"If I can see," I say again.

But I cannot see, I cannot see anything but doubleheaders, and they send me upstairs to a private room.

And a nurse on the floor looks in and says, "The phone's been ringing all morning. One woman called and said, 'My twelve-year-old wouldn't forgive me if I didn't call and find out how Frank was.'"

Frank could be better. I spend another night in the hospital and then they release me with the warning that I am not to read, nor to watch television, that I am to stay in bed and rest.

And I do that, waiting for the double vision to clear and the headache to stop, so that I can go out and play ball again, which is the only thing I know how to do.

But that leaves me plenty of time to sleep, to rest, to think. Lots of time to think.

2 *The Way I Play the Game*

"They always talk about Cobb playing dirty," Sam Crawford said, "trying to spike guys and all. Cobb never tried to spike anybody. The baseline belongs to the runner. If the infielders get in the way, that's their lookout."

From "The Glory of Their Times"

I know in my heart, even as my mind remains a blank about the incident, that I didn't go into second base that night in June of 1967 to try and cut Al Weis, or maim him, or deliberately tear up his knee. I have never in my life gone into someone deliberately to cut him. I went in there to break up the double play, that was the prime consideration. Hard-nosed, no-nonsense baseball. That's the way I've always played the game. That's the way I'll continue to play the game.

It has meant personal sacrifice, however. I have, throughout my career, been called all kinds of names by opposing ballplayers. One guy said I was "deliberately vicious." Another accused me of "trying to maim people." A third said, "I hated his guts when I played against him." Okay, that's their privilege. A lot of this, I think, came because the players didn't know me. To get to know a player, you have to play with him. But that never bothered me. I hate, too. I hate all the fellows around the league who are wearing the other uniform. I hate them while we're playing against them, but then it ends.

I don't like so much what's going on in baseball today, this friendliness between opposing players. I think there's altogether too much of it. Say a buddy of yours is playing shortstop for the other side and you're going out to dinner with him after the game. Then, during the game, you're on first base and a ground ball is hit and your buddy is coming across to tag the bag. You're not going to knock him down. You're not going to hit him to break up the double play. You're just going to slide in nicely, get up, dust off your pants, and go back to the dugout.

I have seen times when a pitcher, a buddy of the batter's, will say to the guy the first time up (the batter may be in a slump or something), "I'll throw you a fast ball." They've done it—not many times, but they have done it.

I don't buy it. I don't buy all this friendliness, all this standing around on the field chatting, all this socializing as if baseball were a popularity contest. It isn't. The idea is to beat these guys, and the tiger just isn't in you when you've got buddies out there, wearing the other uniform.

At the end of the 1965 season I told Chico Cardenas, our shortstop on the Cincinnati Reds: "If I'm traded this year, look out. I'll be in that gray uniform, Chico, so you better get out of my way when I come into second base because I'll take you out." I said it in a joking way, but I meant it. If Vada Pinson, who is my best friend in baseball, were playing shortstop for the Minnesota Twins, I'd go in on him and try to take him out on the play.

One time I spiked Don Zimmer when he was with the Dodgers. He was coming across the bag, out of position actually, on a double play, and I took him out. After the inning, Duke Snider passed me coming in and snarled, "What are you trying to prove?"

I couldn't believe it. I couldn't imagine a big-leaguer, a guy with Snider's ability and hustle, asking me a question like that on a good, hard slide.

I was sorry I had cut Zimmer, but I wasn't going to stand on the field and apologize to him. The next day I did ask how he was, but that was it. I believe that the player should realize the risks involved in his position and he should be able to accept it. The player who's sliding in has a job to do. The majority of the good infielders accept this.

But misunderstandings can occur. In 1960 I got into one of only two fights in my career, and it was over a sliding incident, a misunderstanding on the part of the infielder.

We were playing Milwaukee in a doubleheader at home. In the seventh inning I hit a blooper down the first-base line and it fell inside the line and rolled down into the bullpen. I hustled around first, looked over my shoulder to see how far I could go, and made up my mind that I could make it to third. So I put my head down and went into second base and headed for third.

First baseman Joe Adcock picked up the ball and threw it into third. Ed Mathews, the third baseman, came up from his position toward second base, toward me, and took the throw. I did what any ballplayer would do. I slid. And, naturally, I hit him hard because he was in the baseline.

I went in feet first and put my hands over my face. I thought he might tag me in the face with the swing of his glove, completely by accident. And that's what he did. He got me in the nose and it started to bleed.

I didn't think anything about it. I was out. I got up, started to remove my helmet, and Mathews said, "Cut that out, you ———." I turned around and said something back to him, and that's when he hit me.

He caught me on the side of the face, under the right eye, on the cheekbone. Then he jumped on me and we scuffled on the ground. I was trying to defend myself and get to hit him back, but I never did. The coaches and players came out and broke it up.

I came out of it with the bloody nose, a bruised cheekbone, a cut lower lip, a bruised thumb, and an almost completely closed eye. Mathews was thrown out of the game and I *had* to leave; I wasn't in any condition to continue.

Between games, manager Fred Hutchinson took a look at me. "You can't play, can you?"

"I can."

"Do you want to?"

"Yes," I said.

I went out on the field before the second game and Vada looked at me. I was a mess and I knew what he was thinking. I said, "I'm gonna play."

He said, "Are you serious?" I just smiled at him. I had to play, that's all, I had to play.

And I did. I couldn't see out of the right eye, and a couple of times when I was at bat I had to call time and put a gauze up my nose to stop the bleeding. But I had a good game—a walk, hit by a pitch, a single, a double, and a two-run home run. I also made a good catch, off Mr. Mathews himself. He hit one deep down the left-field line. Just as I got there I flipped into the box seats, and held on to the ball. We beat Milwaukee, 4–0.

In the seventh inning of that game I reached third base and Mathews said to me, "I'm sorry it happened."

I said, "Forget it. I understand."

Baseball is a two-way street, you know. For every time I have cut someone on a slide, I have gotten cut in return. Al Weis tears up his ligaments, I tear up my head. My arms and hands and legs are full of scars caused by spike wounds. I have a big one, five inches long, on my left arm and it came from an unsuccessful attempt to steal home against Pittsburgh. Dan Kravitz was catching and I went in head first and he just stepped on my arm. It was an accident and I felt I was safe and I was up there arguing for four or five minutes. I didn't even know I was cut until someone hollered, "Hey, you're bleeding." I stopped and looked, and it was open up pretty good. In fact, I have three scars from that one incident alone—one on the forearm, one just above the elbow, and one underneath.

I've got another bad scar on my left hand that was caused by a home-plate collision. I slid in and tagged the plate with my hand and the ball got by the catcher. He turned to go after the ball and he stepped on my hand.

I've got a few more, too, here and there, where second basemen have gone up in the air and come down on me. The most lavish scar of all came in September of 1963 when we were playing the Mets. I was on first and the next batter hit the ball in the hole. The shortstop went over and made a good play. Ron Hunt, the Mets' second baseman, was just coming across the bag when I slid trying to break up the double play. Hunt went up in the air to avoid my slide. He came down on my left arm and his spikes punctured my bicep.

I didn't know I was cut until I got up. I looked down and the sweatshirt was torn and I took a peep inside and saw I was laid open. The doctor told me later that if the cut had been an inch or so lower it would have been the end of my career because it would have hit right where the arm bends. As it was it took thirty stitches to close the wound and then they said, "Well, you're through for the season." Ten days later I was back in the lineup. I think if I played the game differently, with a little less recklessness, I would have avoided some injuries. But that's not the way I play the game.

My own personal philosophy is that the game should be played to win at all times. That's why, when I first came up to the major leagues in 1956, I felt I needed something extra to go against the experienced pitchers, and so I changed my stance. I was coming into the majors against pitchers who were much smarter than me. I knew they had pinpoint control, especially on their breaking pitches. I didn't want to give them the complete plate to shoot at. I decided to move up closer and not give the pitchers the outside corner. And I hung my head in there.

So I get hit a lot, sometimes by accident, sometimes by design. Through the 1966 season I had been hit 128 times. In six of my ten years in the National League I led the league in being hit by the pitcher. Four times I was hit on the head. Ruben Gomez, then with the Giants, was the first one to do it, in 1957. And he did it deliberately. The first time up I had tripled off him, the second time I doubled, the third time up, his first pitch hit me on the head.

I stayed in the hospital after that one (though I played the next day) and had several other visits to the hospital after being hit on the head. The worst blow came in 1958 when Camilo Pascual hit me in a preseason exhibition game. That was an accident but it left me shaken and in fear for half a year before I snapped out of it.

Even today, I often think about being hit on the head again. I think that there may come a time when I get hit on the head and I won't bounce back. I may never come out of it. I think about it often, but I try to push it out of my mind because that's one thing a hitter should not think about when he's at the plate.

But in all the times I have been hit by a pitcher, all the times I have purposely been hit, I have never run to any teammate for protection. I have gone to pitchers on our club and told them to strike back when one of our guys was hit—and my managers have said the same—but never when I was the only one hit.

This was one of the things that bugged me early in 1967 when we were losing game after game. We weren't striking back at the opposition. In one game, California pitcher Jim Coates threw at my head—I know he did—and our pitcher said, "We owe him one." But then Coates was out of the game, then out of the league, and we wound up still owing him one. In another game after I hit a home run, Dennis Bennett of the Red Sox hit Brooks in the ribs. Bennett got taken out before it was his turn to bat and we owed him one, too, only he was traded into the National League. In a third game, Jack Sanford hit Andy Etchebarren after Davey Johnson had gotten a hit, and nobody retaliated. The opposition was doing these things and getting away with it and the word was getting out around the league, "The Orioles don't knock our hitters down."

I remember one time a few years ago when our manager told our starting pitcher during a game to flatten the first hitter he faced. This was because I had been knocked flat by their pitcher. Well, he faced the first batter and didn't knock him down. Gene Freese, who was playing third for us, called time and came over to the pitcher.

"Don't look now," he said, "but Robby's heading in for you."

I had started in a few steps but only as a reminder to the pitcher, that's all. Our pitcher turned around, pretending to be rubbing up the ball, and nodded at me. His next pitch caught the batter in the ribs.

In 1965 we were playing the Mets at Shea Stadium and they were giving us a hard time. Roy McMillan, especially, was killing us. He was batting .230 on the year and hitting almost .700 on us. And in this game he had two singles and a home run off Joe Nuxhall. Joe was really mad, but what did he do? After McMillan hit the homer he knocked down the next batter, Johnny Lewis.

That made me mad. I was mad because the Mets were beating us. I was mad Nuxhall had knocked Lewis down instead of McMillan, who had been tormenting us. In the dugout I yapped at Nuxhall, "That isn't the guy you should be knocking down. You should be knocking McMillan down."

He jumped at me and said, "I'll knock down who I want to. Don't you tell me who to knock down."

"That's not the point," I said. "That guy's killing us and nobody's doing anything about it." We were mad at each other for about two minutes, then it was forgotten.

It all comes from not wanting to lose. I do not like to lose. In fact, I cannot stand to lose. I only play to win. Winning always comes first with me. I think my individual performance comes second, at least I try to think that way but maybe I am fooling myself.

Everyone has pride in his own performance, and there are

ballplayers who put their own performance above that of the team's. If I do that at times, it's only because I feel that if I do my job the way I'm expected to, it is taking the pressure off someone else—and it is setting an example. If I steal a base with a head-first slide, or kick the ball out of a fielder's glove, or take a base on a short passed ball, or stretch a single into a double—if I do these things and the kids on our ball club are inspired to play the same way, well, fine. The whole team gets a lift. Personal performance, for me at least, is tied in with winning. That's all that matters.

Baseball, really, is all that matters with me. It's what my life is all about. I have a lovely, understanding wife, and two beautiful children and a happy home life. My family helps complete me as a human being, but I don't know what I'd do or where I'd be without baseball.

It's been that way ever since I was a boy raising strawberries on my backside from sliding on the asphalt playgrounds that passed for baseball diamonds in my ghetto neighborhood. As long as I remember, I wanted to be a baseball player. And I always wanted to be the best. Although I knew I wasn't always the best, I wanted to be and I worked hard at it, and I still do.

I work at nothing else as a matter of fact. Most ballplayers have jobs or their own businesses in the off-season. Not me. I think it would take something away from my baseball, worrying whether the business was doing well or not. A lot of people have said to me, you should get into something now, you're making good money and you'll have it when you get out of baseball. But I can't see it that way. My life is baseball and I think it deserves all my attention.

It's the same even with my leisure. I go to movies in season, I attend pro and college basketball and football games in the off-season because I love all sports. But I don't have any special interests that I think might distract me from the game. I don't read books. I don't play golf. I don't hunt or fish. I simply don't want to get involved in anything but baseball.

Years ago when I was a young man with Cincinnati, the NAACP came to me and asked me to join their organization. I told them I would be glad to join but under one condition. I said that as long as I was in baseball they were not to call on me to make any appearances or anything as far as their cause was concerned. And that's been my policy ever since. A lot of the Negro groups have criticized me for it, because when they call me to lead marches and protests or make personal appearances I have to tell them no. I sympathize with them, really. They've done a great deal of good; I agree with them on some points and there are some points I disagree with them. But I don't think baseball should be a fight for anything but baseball.

That doesn't mean I'm unaware of what's going on in this world, or that it has no effect on me as a person. I'll never forget the first time I met discrimination. It was in 1953, my first year in professional baseball, in Ogden, Utah. I was brought up in California, in Oakland, and while we lived in a predominantly Negro area, I was never aware of any outright discrimination. I just never thought about it. And I think that came from my family . . . my mother, my sisters, my brothers. I never heard any of them ever say, "that white man," or "this colored man." There was just never that type of talk around the house. And I never faced a situation where I was put down because I was a Negro.

But one of my first days in Ogden, I went to the local movie house and the cashier said to me, "I'm sorry but we don't patronize Negroes."

That was the start of it, and it has touched my life ever since—from my playing days in the South to today, trying to get my family decent homes in good neighborhoods.

I'll always remember one incident in 1954 when I was playing for Columbia, South Carolina. Ernie White was our manager and we were playing the Savannah, Georgia, team. Before the game White was running down their lineup. And he came to a fellow who was 6-6 or 6-7 and weighed 240 pounds and was hitting the ball out of sight. White got right to the point.

He said, "How are we going to pitch to this big black nigger?"

A deathly quiet settled over the clubhouse—I was one of two Negroes on our team—but White, who is a Southerner, didn't realize what was going on. That was just his way and he didn't mean anything by it. Sometime later when I tried to go into the stands after three drunken white guys who had been taunting me with foul racial remarks, White stopped me and said, "What happened?"

I told him and he said, "Tell me who they are. I'll go get them for you."

That was the way it was in those days, but it has gotten a lot better. In the old days we didn't socialize off the field, we were never invited anyplace by the white players or anything like that. But now you'll find that fellows are inviting each other to movies and theaters and clubs. And the thinking now is different. I think race prejudice is slowly, slowly being pushed out of baseball, that each individual is coming more and more to be judged not on the color of his skin, but what he is as a man.

I know it was that way with the Orioles in 1966, the year we won our pennant and world championship, the happiest year of my life. There were certain players I could joke with and call "Paleface," and they accepted it as a joke. Once that summer we were coming in to Chicago to play the White Sox. This was at the time of the rioting in Chicago and most of the white players said they were going to stick with the Negro players while they were in Chicago. I said no they weren't—they weren't going to stick with me. I was going to stay away from them. They weren't going to get me shot up.

Driving in from the airport to our hotel, the guys said, "Come on, Robby, get up to the window so they can see you."

I said, "No, thank you." And I stretched down on the floor of the bus—right in the aisle. "Baby," I said, "you're all on your own."

So you see, there is a lot less self-consciousness about race than there once was (though there is still a long way to go). And I'm all for it and I regret, in a way, that I can't be more active, more stand-up. But it would take away from my game.

The way I play the game, I can't be distracted. I always have to drive myself as hard as I can. I can't relax, either. I know that if I'm relaxed, I'm not going to perform as well.

And I try to perform at my peak at all times because I feel this is the only way to be true to the game I love. There is a lot of talk today that changes have to be made in baseball, that it's not exciting enough any more for our times. I don't believe that for a moment. I think the game of baseball is the most exciting game of them all.

I love everything about it. I like playing the outfield, I like to make a good defensive play in the outfield, or wherever I'm playing. It gives me as much satisfaction to throw a runner out as it does to hit a home run. I like to run the bases, to take the extra base, to steal the base. I like to slide and I like to hit. But that's not the only thing I like to do. I like to do all of it, and also I like to watch the fellows on the other ball clubs, and to watch my own players perform. Exciting baseball is made by the players down on the field.

Baseball, all my life, has been the most exciting and fulfilling of all games. I could have played football, I could have played basketball, but baseball was my game. It didn't always go smoothly with me. I have had, I suppose, more than my share of troubles in baseball. I have been called many names by many people. I have had moments when playing baseball for a living wasn't fun. But, somehow, the fun always came back and the bad moments, like bad memories, were forgotten.

Now I try to remember all those moments, the good and the bad. Now I try to look back and piece it all together, and the wonder of it is that it turns out to be a man's life.

3 Dragging around a Bat

Oakland wasn't exactly known as the garden spot of the U.S.A. when I was growing up there in the 1940s, and its reputation hasn't improved much since then. It's still a place to live if you can't afford Berkeley or San Francisco or any of the other middle-class suburbs in the Bay Area. Now Oakland's official population is four hundred thousand, but there are really more than two million people in the area, which is known as the East Bay. It was recently described as a "noisy, ugly, mean-spirited place . . . a natural environment for hoodlums, brawlers, teen-age gangs and racial tensions." Well, I don't think it was that bad when I was a kid living there. I still remember Oakland with affection because, first, it was my home and, second, it never got in the way of what I wanted to do. My life in those days, as it is now, was made of unequal parts that all spelled b-a-s-e-b-a-l-l—baseball, from morning to night.

Ask my mother. I'd go out early in the morning, maybe come home for lunch, then stay out till seven, eight, nine, ten at night, until it got dark. I'd come racing home with the moon and go to the oven and pull out whatever was left for me to eat. Mom would be waiting, and chiding. "Why do you want to be out so late?"

"Playing ball."

She'd sigh, "It's too dark to see."

"Mom," I'd say, "we played until we couldn't see at all." As if she didn't understand.

Later, when I got a little older, she kept after me to go to work. But I couldn't see it. I said, "Ma, I don't want to work. I want to play ball."

So she let me play ball, but then when I needed fifty cents to go to the Roxy or Broadway Theater I always ran into a little trouble. And that meant I ran into trouble every Sunday because Sunday afternoon was movie day for me. I was, and am today, a moviegoer. I mean, a moviegoer. Sometimes they showed three movies on Sunday—a triple feature—plus the serial (Zorro or Captain Midnight or the Green Hornet), and I used to stay and see them all, and see them over and over again, two or three times if I could. I could spend all day in the movies.

But there was this little problem about money, and I'd have to come around to mom, patting her and wheedling, "Gimme fifty cents."

Finally, she'd give it to me and I'd smile at her and say, "Someday, Ma, I'm gonna get rich playing baseball and I'll make you rich."

"Frank," she'd say to me, "I'll be dead and gone to glory before that ever happens."

But she was wrong and I'm thankful for that. She's alive and healthy today, still living in East Oakland, in the house she bought when I was sixteen, still enjoying life and, I think, still getting a kick out of what's happened to me.

She calls herself Ruth Shaw, after the name of her first husband, Burton Shaw, who was a railroad man from Silsbee, Texas. Our family roots are buried deep in that hard-scrabble soil of East Texas. Mom had two other marriages, to Johnny Grisby, who worked for a lumber company in Texas, and Frank Robinson, my father, a railroad man, now deceased.

I was the last of Mom's ten children, who were spread from the top to the bottom, over twenty-five years. I was born in a hospital in Beaumont, Texas, on August 31, 1935, the only child to come out of mom's union with Frank Robinson.

I really don't remember much about my father because he and my mother broke up when I was still a baby. Silsbee, Texas, is a small town just twenty miles north of Beaumont. It's a railroad town and I guess that's why they told me my father worked for a railroad. But all I can remember is him never working for a railroad. He had other things going for him. He was part owner of a funeral parlor, part owner of a grocery store, and he owned quite a number of houses and a lot of land.

He certainly wasn't a real father to me. I don't think anyone can be a real father when he doesn't spend any time at home with his family. But he did come around every now and then, even after he left mom. I remember he taught me how to tie my shoes and he would give me rewards for counting from one to one hundred, and things like that, and he was always concerned about how we were doing.

But then, when I was four, we left Silsbee for California and I never saw him again. The next thing I heard anything about him was 1953 when someone in Silsbee wrote my mother and told her that he had passed away. They asked me to come down to settle up his estate, which was in a real turmoil. I didn't want to go because by then I had no feelings for my father, but my mother made me. So I went back to Silsbee and worked with a lawyer there to settle his affairs, and I got out as soon as I could.

There's only one other thing I remember about my father. When I began playing baseball in high school and started doing well, my older brothers would return from Texas from a visit and tell me what my father had said to them. What he said was: "Frank will never make a big-league baseball player, there's no way he can make it. He'll never live to see the big leagues." I really don't know why he talked that way —maybe out of envy or jealousy that I really did have a chance to make it, or maybe from regret over his never being a real father to me—but it really didn't matter to me because, as I said, by then my father meant nothing to me.

There were three of us kids living in a large, one-floor house in Silsbee with mom. There was Johnny, who was three years older than me, and Sylvester, who was six years older. The other four boys and three girls were almost a generation older than me and they had already gone to California. Then Johnny went to live in Austin with one of my sisters and Sylvester and myself were the only ones at home with my mother. By this time, mom's older children were anxious for us to come out to California. They kept writing mom, telling her of the better opportunities in the Oakland area. So, finally, she did pick up and move to California. And a year or so later, Johnny came out to join us.

At first, we lived in Alameda, which is in the same bay area as Oakland. We lived in a two-bedroom apartment in a small project house with my sister Robertha and her husband, Willie. At that time Robertha worked nights and Willie days in the shipyard and they didn't see each other much, but it made for bed space. I shared the same bed with Sylvester and Johnny.

It wasn't what you would call gracious living but we made out all right. As far as I knew we always had enough to eat in those days. Of course I was quite young and what I call enough to eat might not have been enough to eat for grownups. But I can remember that it was enough for me.

I first started going to school in Alameda; I went to the first and second grades there. The school was on split sessions and I went from twelve to four in the afternoon. I didn't like that very much because those were the hours you got out to play with the kids. I didn't have much of an opportunity to play because of that schedule. Still, I enjoyed school at the time.

We lived in Alameda two years, then we moved in to West Oakland with an older brother, Ellyon (we always called him "Baby"—don't ask me why) and his wife, Roxy. Ellyon worked for a paint company and Roxy worked for the Southern Pacific Railroad. Mom worked then too, mostly at odd jobs. She was getting an allotment from her oldest son, Raymond Shaw, who was in the service, and that helped. There were five people in the house and it was rotating beds again. It was a tight squeeze—we all slept together—but no one ever missed any meals.

Then we made another move to our own three-room apartment at 1515 Myrtle Street in West Oakland, and that's the area where I really grew up. It was in a rough, mixed neighborhood, mostly Negroes but also Mexicans and a lot of Orientals. It wasn't a bad, Harlem-type ghetto and there was never any trouble over race. We all got along pretty good together. As I said I never ran into any problem over being a Negro until my first year in the minor leagues, in the northern city of Ogden, Utah.

Our street itself wasn't too bad; it was like most of the streets in West Oakland, rows and rows of two-story tenement houses. But only a few blocks away it was very rough. We lived between Third and Fourth Streets, and Seventh Street was where the action was—crap games, pool halls, card tables, gangs, fights, and a lot worse. A kid could go either way in this neighborhood. If he wanted to go right, it was there for him. If he wanted to go bad, it was there, too. I chose my own way. I chose not to run with gangs because I was a loner. I was a kid who always ran by himself.

I can only remember two occasions when I got into what you would call real trouble. One day when I was in grade school, I was going home for lunch. Suddenly, this one kid who was supposed to be the big man in the school, stopped me and challenged me. He put his dog on me and I kicked his dog, and I kicked him again and, finally, I hurt the dog and the dog backed off. Then this kid's friend said, "You're not going to let him do that to your dog, are you?"

"Nah," the big man said, and he pulled a knife on me and we had a little scuffle. I came out on the long end of that fight and didn't get hurt. Neither one of us got hurt, actually, and that was the end of it.

The other time was at school when we were kidding and teasing a boy. We were passing his cap around in a big ring and after the passing stopped, I was standing with his cap and he pushed me. I pushed him back and we started to fight. He reported me to the teacher and I had to bring my mother to school the next day to straighten it out.

I was twelve at the time and by now things were getting better for mom. Sylvester had graduated from high school and was working as a civilian storekeeper at the Naval Air Station in Alameda, and he contributed money to the family. Later, Johnny went to work in the canneries. Today, Sylvester works at a government lab in Livermore, California. He's married and has three boys and mom does a lot of baby-sitting for him. Johnny is a career man in the Air Force, currently stationed at Scott Air Force Base in Illinois. He's married, too, and has three girls.

Johnny and Sylvester were both good athletes in high school. They played basketball and ran track and might have made something of themselves in sports, but both had to go to work. I was the lucky one. Being the youngest in the family, I got the breaks.

The only job I ever really had until I got into professional baseball was delivering newspapers. I could earn up to six dollars a week, but I really didn't go about it in a very businesslike way. A lot of times when a baseball game came up, I would get one of my friends to take my route and throw the papers while I played baseball. I had a close friend, George Johnson, who was always very obliging about this. In fact, when the circulation man used to call my house because I wasn't putting out my papers, my mother would always tell him, "You best see George."

You see, baseball already was my life. I liked all sports. As a kid I played baseball, basketball, and football in the playground, and when it was too dark to play outside we'd go into the gym and play baseball or kickball or Ping-Pong or something like that. The gym opened when the playground closed, at six, and we'd play inside until the gym closed, about ten. Sometimes when we didn't have enough kids, we'd play kickball four on a side.

But these other sports were always fill-ins for me, a way to pass the time until we got going on baseball again. I always favored baseball, the challenge of it, the bat and ball, the fielding part of it. Baseball seemed to bring out my competitive instincts more than anything else, and I was always good at it. But I still had to work pretty hard at baseball, just as I do right now and have done since I became a professional.

I think I held a bat in my hand before I could talk. I know my mother says she bought me a baseball bat and mitt when I was just a year old. She said I used to lose all my toys but that I never lost that bat, that I'd drag it around everywhere. I believe her. As far as I can remember, I was always dragging around a bat. I don't know who put it in my hand, but I always had one. Even back in Silsbee, when I was two, three years old, I was playing a lot of stickball in the street. We played with a broomstick and a tennis ball or a rag ball. I can remember that. Then, when we moved to Oakland, I played seven days a week. I'd play with golf balls, tennis balls, balls made of stockings or rags, softballs—anything that was round enough for me to swing a stick at.

In our section of Oakland at that time there wasn't anyplace to play baseball, no diamonds, no grass, no room, so we played at the Tompkins Street School playground, on asphalt. That didn't matter. Right from the first, I'd play all-out. I'd slide in on the asphalt and never think about it. If I raised a strawberry on my backside, I'd just go home and bandage it up and . . . here we go again. Once I tore the whole side of my pants sliding and when my mother saw me she nearly had a fit.

But she was always indulgent to me. I never remember really wanting for anything. I was always well fed and well clothed. Nothing fancy, mind you, but I was warm and had clothes to wear each day and always plenty of food. I never wanted much for myself in those days, anyway. When I got into high school I began to realize some of the things I was

missing. I didn't have as much money to spend as some of
the kids and I wasn't able to buy some of the things in
high school that the high school kids would buy. It took me
a while to save up for the high school sweater, and I didn't
come up with a class ring when I graduated, but when I
really needed something, mom saw that I got it.

I didn't own my first glove until I was fourteen and playing
American Legion ball. I told my mother that I wanted a glove
and she said, okay, and she got me the glove. I'm sure she
found it hard digging up the money for that glove but she
did it. It was her way of encouraging me in baseball.

The only time I ever remember her hitting me was one
day when I was seven or eight and I stuck a bobby pin into
an electric plug. There was a pop and a flash of fire but I
wasn't hurt. The reason she spanked me then, I'm sure, was
out of fright more than anything else. Most of the times when
she was mad at me she'd just talk to me. She'd never raise
a hand. But sometimes she got me wishing she had belted me.
She got me feeling I let her down.

Mom always took good care of all her kids but, I guess
being the youngest, I got more than the others. I could understand it if my brothers felt bitter about me getting away
without working or doing anything but playing ball, but
they never were. In fact, when they had time they'd come
out and play with me. One day they introduced me to the
position of catcher, and I'm glad they did that early in my
life because it quickly cured me of any secret ambitions I
might have had of becoming a Bill Dickey or a Roy Campa-
nella.

It was a Saturday and I was playing with them and a
bunch of older boys. They were shy a catcher so they made
me the catcher. I was only twelve years old but I was tall for
my age and always able to play with kids older than myself.
But catching was a different story. These fifteen-, sixteen-,
seventeen-year-old kids just ran over me at home plate. Fi-

nally, I got so disgusted that I took off the gear, put it down on the ground, and never picked it up again.

All this time, I never let schoolwork interfere with sports. I was an average student but I know I could have done better if I'd put my mind to it. But I was very interested in sports and I just didn't apply myself to schoolwork as much as I should have. I hardly ever brought home homework. I tried to do it all at school because I didn't want it to interfere with whatever sport I was playing after school. It may sound funny after confessing all of this but I did love school. When I was going to the Tompkins elementary school I just hated to see summer vacations come. That meant all the kids would go their separate ways and there wouldn't be as much sports activity with the kids gone. Oh, we did have neighborhood kids around, but there weren't enough of them, not enough who wanted to play sports, and I just hated when summer vacations came.

But I always somehow managed to find someone to play sports with. The playgrounds were very well organized and they had different leagues for kids from ages eight to twelve, something like the Little League. The playgrounds furnished the gloves. You just checked the glove out and checked it back in when you were through with it.

I still remember our playground director. Her name was Mary Lou Russo and she lived two blocks from the playground. She was in charge of everything and that made her the most important person in the world to me. In the summer we'd get up early and go over to her house and sit on the steps until she came out. And if we thought she was a little slow we'd bang on the door and say, "Miss Russo, let's go open the schoolyard."

The summer leagues were organized by playground directors like Mary Lou Russo and we played once a week, on Saturday. That was the day I looked forward to. The games would start early in the morning and they would have four or five games a day at this one playground, and I played in as many games and in as many different leagues as I could fit in. And it was playing baseball in these playground leagues that I got to meet the man who was to have such an important influence on my life.

4 "I Understand You Play Ball"

It is not entirely a coincidence, I think, that Oakland—and particularly McClymonds High School—has produced major-league ballplayers far out of proportion to its population. Around my time alone there was Jesse Gonder and Curt Flood and Vada Pinson and Willie Tasby—and in basketball, a fellow named Bill Russell.

Russell, in his book, *Go Up for Glory*, gave as good a reason as any why McClymonds was producing so well. George Powles was his name.

Russell was a year and a half in front of me at McClymonds but I did play part of one season on the basketball varsity with him. He was a big, awkward six-seven then, but already a very tough defensive player. And whatever he was when we played together was 100 percent better than what he was when George Powles first got him.

It was Powles, the basketball and baseball coach at McClymonds, who persuaded Russell to come out for jayvee basketball when Bill was a stringbean sophomore with little coordination. Powles then had fifteen jayvee uniforms and carried sixteen players. Russell was the sixteenth and he shared a uniform with the fifteenth man. "By that one gesture," Russell said in his book, "I believe that man saved me from becoming a juvenile delinquent. If I hadn't had basketball, all of my energies and frustrations would surely have been carried in some other direction."

Nothing so dramatic came out of my relationship with Powles, but this man did have a tremendous influence on my life. He's in his late fifties now, still working with the kids in Oakland, and has never really gotten the credit due him for all he's done over the years for the young men around the city. And I'm not just thinking of the Bill Russells and the Frank Robinsons, who normally get the headlines. I mean all the other ones who didn't quite make it but whose lives were shaped for the better because of Powles.

I had just turned fourteen, a ninth-grader at Westlake Junior High, when I first met Powles. One night in October, Powles was working in the high school gym and some of my friends from Westlake were playing basketball. Powles came up to them. "Who's the best baseball player in your school now?" he asked.

"Frank Robinson," they said.

"Who's he?"

They said, "He comes around to shoot baskets once in a while."

"Well," Powles told them, "have him speak to me the next time he comes around."

My buddies passed the word and about a week later I went over to the gym and introduced myself to Powles. "I'm Frank Robinson," I said. "You wanted to speak to me?"

He must have been about five-feet-nine, around 170, a stocky guy with a friendly, open face. I think I liked him right off. He said, "I understand you play ball."

"That's right."

"I've got this team that plays at Bushrod Park on Sunday mornings, the Doll Drug Company. How'd you like to play with us?"

"Sure would," I said.

"Well, come on up this Sunday."

Bushrod Park is in North Oakland, quite a distance from my house, so I got on my bicycle and made the trip. Most of the kids on the team were fifteen and sixteen years old. But Mr. Powles gave me a uniform right off and sat me on the bench. In the fifth inning he told me to go up and pinch-hit.

I went up there and hit the first pitch over the center fielder's head for a home run. I stayed in the game and got to bat once more, and hit the ball against the left-field fence for a triple. After the game, Mr. Powles said I had made the team.

That spring of 1950 Powles picked me to play on his American Legion team, and I felt it was quite an honor. For one thing, I was the youngest player on the squad. For another, his Bill Erwin Post 237 club had won the national championship the year before, and it was still a team full of fine ballplayers. Something like fourteen of the twenty-five kids on the two-year roster signed contracts and played professional baseball. The big guy on the 1950 team was J. W. Porter, who later signed with the White Sox for a huge bonus. Porter didn't make it in big-league baseball and I could never understand why. I used to marvel at him. He had a real nice, smooth, level swing. He had good power, he had a strong arm, and he was a fine catcher. He must have batted over .500 in Legion ball.

Certainly, he was the star of that '50 Legion team while I was just another player. Powles spotted me in right field, and I'd say I started half the games. I do remember breaking up one game with an extra-inning home run.

We won the local tournament and went to Winslow, Arizona, for the regionals, and I got sick. I began to suffer stomach pains and the doctor diagnosed it as acute appendicitis. I was scared and I guess Mr. Powles was too, because he made plans to fly me home the next day. But that morning another doctor looked at me and he took a blood count and said it wasn't appendicitis, just nerves. I had another attack later when we got to the sectionals in Hastings, Nebraska, and it may have been nerves again. I know I was homesick; I had never been away from home and everything was so strange to me.

Mr. Powles did everything he could to cheer me up. I celebrated my fifteenth birthday in Hastings and he bought a cake for the occasion and we had a little party. That helped. Winning helped, too. We took our three games at Hastings and went on to the finals at Omaha, Nebraska. We won three more and that was it—our second straight national championship. I remember hitting a ball 350 feet off the fence in right-center field in one of those games, which was considered a pretty good hit for a freshly minted fifteen-year-old right-handed hitter.

We came back to Oakland and were met at the train by a mob of fans and everyone was happy and it really was one of the big thrills of my life.

But in some ways I kind of felt out of it. I guess it was that I was so young and that I was only one of two Negroes on the team. I was painfully shy in those days, anyway. George Powles did his best to shake me out of it. He'd invite me over to his house and I'd go in the living room and sit in a chair with my head hanging to the floor, staring down at my lap. Mrs. Powles would come in and say, "Hello, Frank," and I'd say hello and never look up. But then we'd start to talk baseball and it would be all right. We'd talk for hours, maybe three or four days a week. That was a real baseball house.

I was a tall, gangling, skinny kid at the time. My mother used to get on me all the time because I slouched. "Straighten your shoulders up! Straighten your back up! Look like a man!" she'd say, but I guess that was my natural posture because it hasn't changed a bit to this day. People see me walk and say that I look like I'm aching all over. But I've always walked that way, always moved that way, and when people tell me about it now, I just tell them that I'm conserving my energy until I need it. I've been criticized for it, but that's just the way I am.

I was concerned about my physique, though, and so was Powles. "If you want to be a big-league ballplayer," he said to me one day, "you've got to build yourself up." And he gave me some exercises to do, including pushups and different things to strengthen my forearms, my arms and back. I took to squeezing a rubber ball to build up my wrists and every day I'd go home and exercise. I remember I started doing ten pushups at a time and worked myself up until I could do a hundred.

About a month after I started this routine, the coach came over to check on me. "You doing your exercises?" he asked.

I said, "Oh, yes, I'm doing them."

I don't know that he believed me for he turned to my brother, Sylvester. "What about it, Sylvester, is it true?"

Syl said, "That boy is shaking the house down. He just won't stop with those exercises."

I entered McClymonds High in the fall of 1950 and I enjoyed my days there. McClymonds, which is in West Oakland, had about nine hundred students then, mostly Negro. The other high schools in the city were a lot bigger, but our sports teams were usually the best in the city.

I made the baseball team as a sophomore, and became a regular in basketball when I was a junior. We had an outstanding basketball team. I was six-one at the time but couldn't play forward because I was considered too small. We had fellows six-three and six-four playing forward, and Bill Russell was the center, and we won two northern California championships with Russell. He graduated in January of my junior year and after that we didn't do quite as well. In my senior year, I averaged about fifteen points a game, mostly from the outside, and made All-City.

In the fall of my junior year I decided to give football a try. It wasn't much of a try. My career lasted two plays.

Actually, I never enjoyed football that much. Football and basketball for me were things to do while waiting for the baseball season. And I never worked at these sports the way I always worked at baseball. I did enjoy playing playground football when I was a kid, but when it came to organized football, I wasn't too keen on it. I think it was that I didn't want to apply myself to learning all the plays. My mother was always against my playing football, anyway, but I finally talked her into it, and I made the team as a defensive back.

Our first competition that fall was in an exhibition game against Richmond High. I didn't start the game, but they were running around right end pretty good and the coach put me in at defensive back and I did all right. Our next game was the preseason football jamboree. That's when all the Oakland high schools play the same night, the East Oakland schools playing against the West Oakland schools. We scored first and then we lined up for the kickoff. One of my team-mates said, "Let's go down and get 'em," and that's just what I did. I went storming downfield and made the tackle. Only I didn't get up. I lay on the ground holding my right shoulder.

It hurt bad but the worst of it was that I couldn't move my right shoulder or arm. It felt paralyzed. The ambulance came in through the gate and carted me off and I cried all the way to the hospital. I cried not so much because I was hurt but because I thought I had ruined my arm for baseball.

Powles jumped in his car and followed the ambulance to the hospital. The X-rays turned out negative. I guess it was shock more than anything because the shoulder came right around.

The following week I was back in our starting lineup against Fremont. On the first play their left end caught a pass near me. Instead of coming in and hitting him with my right shoulder, which was still sore, I tried to let him go by me so I could tackle him on the left side. It didn't work. He went by me and his cleat came up and gouged me between the eyes, opening up a bad cut. Blood came streaming out and I left the game.

They bandaged me up and I went home and sat down alone to dinner. My mother came in the door and my back was to her. She said, "How'd it go?"

I turned around and she caught one look at me with one eye closed, my face all bandaged up, and she let out a little moan.

"It's all right, Ma," I said, "I'm through with football."
And I was. I just counted my blessings and turned in my uniform.

So between basketball, that interlude in football, and baseball, I found myself with barely enough time for schoolwork. I wasn't a very good student, anyway, because I never felt schoolwork was that important. I knew what I was going to be—a professional baseball player—and that was it. And if it hadn't been for one teacher at McClymonds, Miss Grace Johnstone, I don't know if I would have graduated. She straightened me out as much as anyone in my life. Without her support, without her faith in me, I might not have made it to where I am now.

But it didn't start out that way. No, it didn't. Before the second semester of my sophomore year, I was talking over my program with my counseler. She suggested I take a crafts course.

"Crafts?" I said. "I don't want to take that."

I was against it. I wasn't going to take it, and that was it. But I needed something to fill out my schedule, so I finally gave in.

The crafts teacher was Grace Johnstone, who had just transferred to McClymonds from junior high, where she had taught phys ed to girls. And we got off on the wrong foot right away, because I didn't want to be in that class and anything I could do to make it uneasy for the teacher, I was going to do.

At that time I was a real smart kid, and by that I mean a smart alec. I would always come out with wise remarks and, as Miss Johnstone once wrote about me, "for a shy, gentle boy, Frank can be amazingly resistant to doing something he doesn't want to do."

That was the situation in this crafts course. There were twenty-eight of us boys in the crafts room, and I guess I was kind of the ringleader. The room was equipped with all sorts of things to throw at one another, especially nice soft balls of wet clay. And that's what we did that first day, and Grace Johnstone didn't seem to know what to do about it. I don't think she ever experienced anything like us when she was teaching junior high, and at first she was kind of paralyzed.

Things came to a head when the home economics teacher next door came bursting into our room holding a flattened wad of clay. She looked at Miss Johnstone icily. "One of your boys threw this at my monitor in the hall."

That did it. Miss Johnstone went on a sit-down strike. When we got to class the next day, the cupboards were locked and there was a large sign painted on an old window shade she had hung on the wall behind her desk. The sign read: "You can work if you wish, but I will not work with you until certain promises are made and kept." She didn't say one word that whole class. She just sat at her desk pretending to be reading a book.

At first, we got a great kick out of this. We laughed and laughed, and had no more idea of doing any work than the man in the moon. Besides, we didn't have any materials to work with. So we just spent the whole period talking and laughing and joking to each other. All this time, Miss Johnstone never looked up from her book.

The next day it was the same thing only now we weren't laughing. We were beginning to feel restless and bored. One of the kids asked her if they could work on their project. Miss Johnstone looked up coolly and said, "Certainly you may," and continued to read.

We all looked a little puzzled and one kid said, "How? The cupboards are locked." Miss Johnstone continued to ignore us.

The third day, after roll call, she still had her head buried in that book. Quietly, we moved our chairs close to her desk. My chair was in the middle. I was the elected spokesman of the group and I said, "What do we have to do so you'll work with us?"

Her terms were uncompromising. First, the kid who hit the

girl had to apologize to her and to the home economics teacher. Then Miss Johnstone got promises from us that from now on, we would try to behave like human beings. She opened the cupboard and the class went as smoothly as any I'd ever been in.

I got to enjoy that class so much. I liked working with my hands. We soldered silver, polished plastic and stone, carved wood. I remember making a silver ring with Miss Johnstone's help and presenting it to my latest girl friend. But more than the class itself was the chance to establish a friendship with Miss Johnstone. She told someone later, "Once Frank was my friend, everyone was my friend." Well, it wasn't very hard being her friend. She was an unusual woman. She was very patient and understanding with me and helped me out many times when I got into trouble. I felt if I had problems I could consult with her. We became very close my last two years in high school. In fact we got to where we could kid each other.

I'd tell her, "When I sign a major-league contract for seventy-five thousand dollars, I'll buy you a Cadillac."

And she'd come right back. She'd say, "You think you're big enough to be a big-league ballplayer. I don't think so. You just don't have what it takes." She always put me in my place and kept me from getting a swelled head.

There was one time when I decided to grow a mustache. It was a magnificent mustache, I thought, large and flowing, dropping regally down the corners of my mouth. Miss Johnstone took one look at it and started calling me, "Dr. Fu Manchu." The message was clear and I soon shaved it off.

But with all this needling, she could be tough on me when she had to. One day I was supposed to take a biology test, only I decided I didn't want to. I told the teacher and he went to Miss Johnstone; when I got into trouble the teachers preferred going to her rather than the principal. The teacher came back and said to me, "Miss Johnstone says that if you don't take the test, you don't play." We had a regularly scheduled league game and I had never missed a game in my life, but I missed that one. I didn't take the test and I didn't play. I really wanted to play—it killed me inside—but I didn't show it, I couldn't show it. That's the way I was. Besides, I didn't think they'd really keep me from playing.

In my senior year my mother bought a five-room house in East Oakland. It was a step up from the old neighborhood— mostly Negro but some mixed, a little more money, a little better conditions. The trouble was, it was way out of way from McClymonds, over an hour by streetcar. Well, Miss Johnstone lived near us and she would often drive me over to school for dances or night affairs. She and mom became friendly and when Miss Johnstone entertained her A students, mom would go over and help with the refreshments. And Miss Johnstone was very good to us.

That year I wanted to buy my girl an orchid for the senior ball, but I didn't have the money. So Miss Johnstone invited me over to her house to wash her walls. I did, and she paid me and I got the orchid for the girl. That was the kind of woman Grace Johnstone was, and is today. She is retired now but I still hear from her and when I get back to Oakland I try to make it my business to visit her.

George Powles and Grace Johnstone. These were the two people who, outside of my own family, did the most for me when I was growing up. But there was another one who had something to do with what I am today, and his name is Bobby Mattick.

Bobby first noticed me when I was fourteen and playing junior legion ball. He was a scout for the White Sox then and he came around to take a close look at J. W. Porter, and he stayed. He eventually did sign Porter to a White Sox contract at a bonus of sixty-five thousand dollars, and he picked off a few other kids while he was at it.

He seemed to take a liking to me. He was always around and always seemed to be genuinely concerned about my welfare. I remember he had a fit when I went out for football.

When George Powles told him about my injury he rushed over to our house and told my mother never to let me play football again. His mission was pointless since I had no intention of playing any more football, but it was good to know he cared.

And he really did seem to care about me. During the summer, he used to take me out and hit me ground balls. And he came to as many McClymonds games as he could.

I was a third baseman then. My fielding wasn't all that bad. My throwing was. But you couldn't play the outfield in high school. That wasn't the glamorous position. So I played third base.

My senior year I even got to pitch two games when George Powles found himself short on pitchers. I had a fast ball and a curve and in one game I had a shutout going for six innings, but had to be relieved. I ended my pitching career with a 2–0 record.

I batted fourth on our team and my sophomore year I hit .333. My junior year I slipped to .286 and my senior year I batted .424. We won two league championships and I made All-City each of those three years, but that .424 average wasn't even good enough to lead my own team. A teammate of mine, a sophomore, batted .429. Curt Flood.

My batting stance in those days was about like anyone else's. I stood back in the batter's box, my head held almost straight up. I did lean over the plate and hang in with the curve ball, waiting for it to break. I got hit in the head once that way, but it was nothing serious. It came more from not knowing how to get out of the way of the ball. The ball was thrown behind me and I put my head down and the ball hit me on the head. I was out for five minutes. They took me to a hospital, but the X-rays were all negative.

In high school I seemed to get hurt more sliding than anything else. George Powles used to say every time I slid I'd roll on the ground rubbing my knees. But, mostly, I was free of injuries. The high school fields were open fields and you didn't have to worry about fences or walls, and you didn't play that heavy a schedule. We didn't play but ten league games and the chances of injury were very slight.

I learned an awful lot about the game of baseball from George Powles. He was terrific on the fundamentals, but he always went a step beyond them. Powles taught us how to *think* baseball. He taught that if you tried to steal third, you should be able to make it. You should have that positive attitude when you try to steal second, but not as much as third, because at second you're already in scoring position. He taught us that if you tried to take the extra base—third base—you should make it nine times out of ten. He taught us that you should only take a big enough lead off first not to be picked off, and that you should *never* be picked off second base.

One thing he never had to teach me was how to hit with power. He certainly helped by prescribing those exercises that built up my shoulders and arms and wrists, but one thing I could always do was hit with power. I remember one game we played in Berkeley when I hit a ball over the track beyond the outfield, about 380 feet. Another time at Lincoln Park in Alameda, I hit a ball to the opposite field, about 350 feet.

That long-ball hitting attracted other scouts besides Mattick. Doc Bennett of the St. Louis Browns came around and Bill Marshall of the Milwaukee Braves, and there were feelers from the Yankees, Indians, and Oakland.

I had a special affection for Oakland. In the 1940s and early '50s the Pacific Coast League was an outstanding league. As a kid I used to sneak in the ball park to watch the Oakland Oaks. The stands were built over the sidewalk and I'd climb up the side in right field, go through a hole in the fence and then down into the seats. Later George Powles got me a job with Oakland as a ballboy. Brick Laws was running the Oakland team then and he used to ask Powles to tip him off to promising players. Laws would give them jobs around the park to try to get the inside track in case he wanted to sign 'em later. So I got a job.

I enjoyed it, especially being so close to the big stars of the Pacific Coast League. But I was disillusioned. These guys never helped anybody, never answered one question or gave us tips about baseball. I vowed then if I ever made it in baseball I'd always be available to help the kids—if they asked for that help. And if I got out of baseball completely, I would try to work with kids.

Well, I got out of that job quick. There was a guy named Jules Chico in charge and I was late a couple of times and Chico fired me.

That was all right. I doubt very much if I would have signed with Oakland under any circumstances. Bobby Mattick always had the inside track with me and when, in my senior year, he switched to the Cincinnati Reds, I immediately leaned toward Cincinnati. It always frightened me that I might wind up in a large organization—Cleveland or the Yankees—and get lost in the minor-league system. I was determined not to sign with any of them unless they came up with an outstanding bid, and I knew they weren't going to do that.

What it came down to, finally, was Cincinnati and the White Sox. The day I graduated high school the Browns' scout sent me a telegram and told me not to talk to anyone until he got back into town. But I just wasn't interested in the St. Louis Browns.

Both Cincinnati and the White Sox offered me the same bonus—$3500. But the White Sox wanted me to start in Class D and Cincinnati wanted me to start in Class C. Well, I had played on better high school teams and American Legion teams than I would play in Class D, and I told them that and so that was the difference. It made it easier for me to make a decision in favor of the Reds.

Bobby came over to the house one day shortly before my graduation and we discussed my bonus, if that's what you want to call it. He explained that if I took $4000 or more I had to play Triple A ball. If I accepted more than $4000 I had to stay on a big-league roster for two years and sit on the bench one of those years. That was the bonus rule in those days. He offered me the $3500 bonus but also a salary of $400 a month. The average monthly salary in Class C then was $125, so that was a factor.

I had it pretty much figured out, anyway. One, I didn't want to spend one or two years in the big leagues on the bench. Two, I thought it was best for me to start in Class C, that I wasn't ready for a higher classification. Everyone should know what his capabilities are and I felt I knew mine, that I could play C ball, possibly B ball, but that I wasn't ready for Double A ball at that time. I had a lot to learn, I felt I had the ability but had to get the rough edges off. I knew I wasn't a hitter yet, I was a swinger. The curve ball gave me an awful lot of trouble and, save for the fast ball, I had trouble recognizing certain pitches. Class C was just about right for me in June of 1953.

I graduated from McClymonds but delayed signing for a week because I wanted to play in the All-Star game the San Francisco *Examiner* puts on every year, with kids from San Francisco and Oakland playing each other. So I held off and played in that game and right afterward Bobby Mattick came over to the house and I signed my first professional contract.

I gave the $3500 to my mother and she put it in the bank. She was very happy, and so was I. Here I was, seventeen years old, and a whole new life opening for me. I felt—scratch that . . . I *knew*—I was going on to the biggest adventure of my life.

5 _Minor Leagues,_
Major Troubles

I was assigned to Ogden, Utah, in the Pioneer League, and
Bobby Mattick drove me to what seemed at the time to be
another country. Remember, the only time I had left California was on those trips with the American Legion team. It
felt strange going to Ogden. It would be the first time I
would be away from home for any extended period. It was
strange, too, because now I was playing baseball for a living.
Now I was trying to be a big-leaguer one day. I knew that
from now on I would be judged on performance.

The strangeness persisted as I was welcomed to the club,
as I was given a uniform and a locker. It wasn't like starting
out in spring training and making the team. Here it was, the
middle of the season, the ball club was going great (they
were in first place) and here I was, a kid, the youngest member of the club, a stranger among veteran professional ballplayers. And, right away—boom—I was moved into the
lineup.

They chased a very fine third baseman, Carl Palys, out of
the lineup to make room for me. I was feeling very self-
conscious, going up there to bat for the first time as a
professional. But I adjusted quickly. My first at bat I hit a
triple 412 feet off the center-field wall—off a fast ball, naturally.

The next day, I cleared the left-field fence, for my first
professional home run.

It was a good start but kind of misleading. The hitting
part of it was okay, but I was no third baseman. I don't think

I played many games at third for Ogden, but it seemed like I played 164. My fielding was erratic and when I did come up with the ball, my arm was erratic. I just didn't feel at home at third base. I was always tense. So I went up to my manager, Earle Brucker, and I told him to move me off third base.

Brucker was a real good guy. He was a veteran who had played in the majors with the Philadelphia Athletics and he knew how to handle kids. It always seemed that nothing bothered him. He was very patient with the team. But he was puzzled by my request. He said he was very happy with my play at third base. "I'll be glad to try you in the outfield," he said, "but you're dead wrong, Frank, to want to switch just to get away from third."

I persisted. I said, "Look, if they want me to go anywhere in this game of baseball, you better put me in the outfield."

So Brucker said, "Okay, you're my left fielder."

I felt right at home out there, though I had to get used to the fences. In high school you had the open spaces and didn't have to contend with fences. Here, it was a matter of judging the fences, and I wasn't a very good judge in the beginning. My philosophy of playing the outfield then, as it is now, was that I should catch any ball that stayed in the park. That created certain difficulties, but I wasn't worried about getting hurt. I notice today that a lot of ballplayers worry about injuring themselves and try to avoid injuries by shying away from the wall. Well, you can't tell a kid he's got to ram into the wall to catch a ball. It's all up to the individual. Some players will do anything to win, and that's just the way I played the game. I made a few contacts with the left-field fence, but I felt very comfortable and happy out there. I relaxed more and I was able to perform better.

My hitting picked up, too. I remember a girl friend of mine started keeping a scrapbook about me at that time, from clippings I sent her. And very early in my career, she figured out the following:

Frank Robinson 7/20/53

12-Game Hitting Average

Batting	.465
Home Runs	6
Triples	2
Doubles	6
Singles	6

Lord knows, I had plenty of time to cut up the newspapers. All the ballplayers lived in private homes, all but two of us. The two Negro players on the club, Frank Robinson and Chico Terry, had to live in a hotel.

For a northern city, Ogden was extremely southern in some of its viewpoints. There weren't many Negroes living in Ogden. It was a railroad stop, mostly, for Negro porters. And the Negroes were put in their place. There was discrimination in housing and I couldn't go to the movies because I was a Negro. And that hurt me.

The thing was, I had never been exposed to anything like that before. It didn't register with me at the time. I didn't know what really was going on. So I stayed away from the movie house. I played ball, then went down town and shot pool with some of the fellows, or went back to the hotel and rested.

We were quite a combination, Chico Terry and me. I was a frightened kid out of high school, and Chico was a kid who couldn't speak any English. All the way from spring training until he came north, the only thing he could say was "coffee." But we tried to help each other. He helped me with Spanish and I helped him with English. Neither of us learned anything but we got along real well.

On the road it was better. We all stayed in the same hotel. We traveled by bus to Idaho Falls, Pocatello, Billings, Salt Lake City, Great Falls. The trip from Ogden to Great Falls was fifteen hours but none of us minded it. We had a lot of fun on the bus, and we all got along very well together. It was quite an experience visiting that part of the country. Ogden itself was right in the middle of the Wasatch mountain range and you really began to get a feeling of the immensity of this country.

The traveling was an experience, and meeting complete strangers was, too. My trouble was I couldn't relate to people, I couldn't go right up and become friendly with people. It's always been tough for me to meet strangers. I was very shy then and I still am to a certain extent, though I talk more than I used to.

I was very lonely for a while but in late July my mother came up to visit me with Sylvester. They were very proud and wanted to see me play. They stayed three or four days and it really helped break up the season. I had one of my best series when they were there. I hit a couple of home runs and generally played very well.

Earle Brucker made it easy for me, for all of us. He talked a lot of baseball, but he didn't try to change things. He let me alone, figuring experience would be the best teacher. And it was. I always hit pretty well, but I did have shortcomings and weaknesses. I found the pitching a little tougher than high school. Now you were facing pretty good pitching every day instead of once or twice a week. And I still had a lot of trouble with the breaking ball.

I had a lot to learn, too, about the strategy of the game. I learned how to execute the squeeze and the hit-and-run. I learned how to slide correctly. I always thought I knew how to slide, but I didn't. Once I twisted my knee sliding into second base, and I rammed it a few other times. But by the end of the season, I had learned.

Looking back at it, the whole season was a tremendous thrill. Even though I was playing for money, baseball was still fun. We won the championship of the league and I hit .348 in seventy-two games and led the club in home runs (seventeen) and runs batted in (eighty-three). Many years later,

I found out what Brucker wrote the Reds' front office about me after that 1953 season:

"Good speed, fair fielding, great power, great arm, definitely major-league prospect. High-class boy."

High-class boy indeed. I think that's the first time anyone ever called me that.

So the high-class boy went back home after the season, feeling a lot more confident about his chances to make the majors.

I kept in shape that winter by playing semi-pro ball once a week in San Francisco and working out almost every day at Bushrod Park. I wasn't sure where the Reds would be sending me for the 1954 season until the day I got a phone call from Gabe Paul, Cincinnati's general manager.

Paul congratulated me on having a good year and then he got down to business. "Frank," he said, "did you ever stop to think how valuable you would be to the Cincinnati club the way you hit if you were an infielder?"

I muttered, "Uh-huh," thinking of my miserable experience at third base.

"I'd like to assign you to Tulsa next spring and try you at second base. Would you be willing to go along?"

I said, "I like the idea of playing Double A ball, but why at second base? You know what happened to me when I tried to play third."

Paul brushed it off. "Look, we'll be very patient with you. Just think what it would mean to the Reds if we had a power-hitting infielder, a guy who could hit twenty or more home runs a year."

Paul was very persuasive and I agreed to the great experiment and a few days later I received a gift from Gabe Paul, an infielder's glove.

I reported to the Reds' minor-league camp at Douglas, Georgia, and I never worked so hard in my life. It was ground balls, ground balls, ground balls. Joe Schultz, the manager, hit them to me, and Frank McCormick, who had played first base for the Reds, hit them to me, and they never let up. I worked and worked at it. I still didn't like it. I was still having trouble with my arm because it's a different kind of throw in the infield. You throw more with the arm rather than a follow-through with the body; it really took some adjustment. But I stuck with it and I broke camp with the Tulsa team as a second baseman.

My career at Tulsa was brief and to the point—a total of eight games.

We opened up on the road and I got off to a horrible start. I had eight hits, all singles, and I played second base like an amateur magician playing the Palace. After that eighth game, my batting average at .267 (eight for thirty), my fielding average about the same, I got called into the general manager's office. He told me that I was being sent to Columbia, South Carolina, in the Class A Sally League.

He said, "We appreciate the job that you've done here, Frank. It's not that we're not happy with you, but you're just not fancy enough around second base."

That was all right but he made it very clear to me that no matter what I did at Columbia, I wouldn't be back at Tulsa that year. The Cincinnati organization had a policy of not moving its players around during the season. The GM didn't come right out and say so, but my demotion meant that I was stuck at Columbia for the rest of the year, no matter what I did down there. I could hit .700 or .800 but Tulsa wasn't going to bring me back.

I was very disappointed. The team wasn't doing well and someone had to go and I was the logical one, but I didn't think it was entirely fair. First, I was playing out of position at second base. Second, they had stayed with me for only eight ball games. I don't think that was a true test. Third, and worst of all to my way of thinking, they had changed my hitting.

Joe Schultz said I had too big a hitch in my swing. I was

still holding the bat straight up in 1954, and I moved the bat up and down preparing for the swing, and he wanted me to change it to halt the hitch; he wanted me to hold my hands still. I went along with him—I was an eighteen-year-old kid and I wasn't going to talk back, I went along with Schultz even though it ran counter to what Bobby Mattick had once told me. "There'll be fellows wanting to change your style," he said. "Be polite and listen, but let the advice go in one ear and out the other." Well, I couldn't do that with the manager. I had to go along, but it just wasn't the way I could hit. The new swing didn't create any power. I just wasn't pulling the ball at all. I was hitting all the balls to right field.

What Schultz called my hitch was just my way of preparing myself to swing. Each hitter has his own way of preparing himself. I don't think there's a hitter around who doesn't prepare himself by moving a hand or moving the bat some way just when he starts his swing. Each player does it differently—some more drastically than others. Early one spring Leon Wagner was complaining because, he said, he had a flaw in his hitch. A flaw in his hitch. Smoky Burgess, the greatest pinch-hitter in baseball history, had a real deep hitch, but that never bothered him. Jackie Robinson used to hold the bat up quite high, but he didn't hit from there. He had to bring the bat down and his hands down to swing. That was his natural way of swinging. My natural way was to move the bat up and down. I don't care what you do before you swing, as long as you swing into the ball. You can flip the bat in the air if you want to before you swing, just as long as you get the bat back in time to make the proper swing, get the bat back in front of you. When I reported to Columbia, I went back to my old way of swinging.

I caught up with the team at Savannah, Georgia, and in my first game the Savannah pitcher got me out my first three times up. Then the crowd started to get on me. Someone yelled, "You're the guy that came down from Double A. You don't look so strong to me."

My fourth at-bat I hit a home run. The next night against Savannah I had one of my best days ever.

My first time up, I hit a home run over the center-field fence. My second time up, I hit a home run over the left-center-field fence. My third time up, I hit a home run over the left-field fence. My fourth time up, I got the best pitch of the night, a fast ball right down the middle, waist-high. I popped it straight up in the air.

The home crowd at Columbia was very good to me from then on. I mean the white fans as well as the Negroes, even though the local paper did report the following one day: "The customers, 975 of them of Robinson's own Negro race . . ." Well, I said to myself, that's a unique way of reporting a ball game. But I felt it must be a plus factor for me to have Negroes coming out to see me.

You see, there were four Negroes on the Columbia team and it was the first time ever at Columbia, and no one was quite sure how to handle the situation. Off the field of course, the situation was handled according to local custom; that is, strict segregation. There were three movie houses in town and only one admitted Negroes, in the balcony. There were only certain restaurants you could eat in—Negro only —and you certainly couldn't stay where the white players stayed.

But that part was all right. The living conditions in Columbia were very good for us. We stayed in a big white house and Miss Anderson, the owner, kept it spotless. It was really out of place for the neighborhood, a beautiful home with large, clean rooms and double beds. Miss Anderson was a very nice person and we were very fond of her. She was happy-go-lucky, and easy to get along with. And there was a good restaurant right around the corner.

So we didn't mind it much; I roomed with a fellow by the name of John Jackson and since we played most of our games at night, we spent the day in the house resting or writing letters home. You hated to leave that house to go on the road.

That was the worst experience of all playing ball in the South. The home crowd was generally very good, but when you hit the road, that's when you got it. Those fans in Macon and Augusta, Georgia, would give it to us real good. They never let up on us. They always reminded us of the color of our skin. You made an error or did something wrong, they'd start hollering—"Nigger, go back to Africa." Or worse.

I only had one incident on the field that year, though. We were playing Macon at Columbia and I slid into second base and broke up a double play and the second baseman thought I had gone out of the baseline to hit him. He called me a nigger and we started fighting. But they broke it up and nothing came of it.

It was off the field you felt it the most away from home. Let's say you played a Sunday afternoon game at home and you had a Monday game scheduled in Macon. So you took off right after the game and rode all night. The Negro players had to sit on the bus the whole trip. We'd have to stay on the bus while the white fellows went into the restaurant and ordered whatever they wanted. They'd sit down and relax a while and we had to wait until they brought us a sandwich or something out to the bus, and we couldn't even get out to go to the bathroom. And when we got to the town, the white players would go to the local air-conditioned hotel and we'd go either to a private home or to the YMCA. There it was four to a room and no shower and we had to line up to get into the tub. And we had to wait for Negro cabs to take us to the ball park, and we had to go out and look for places to eat, look for a restaurant that would serve us.

I look back at those days now with much less bitterness than I felt at the time. I remember I hated it then. You get angry inside but one person isn't going to throw the thing down. I was a kid and I reasoned at that time that it was part of baseball, and the idea was for me to play baseball.

I just accepted it and made myself a promise that I'd have a good year and get out of there and be done with the South.

And I did have a good year, and I played all-out. One day in Macon I was going after a foul fly. The light poles there were inside the park, down the foul lines. I must have given it a long run of about 150 feet, and all I remember is ramming that pole, full tilt, with my chest. Ernie White, our manager, said later, "He hit the pole hard enough to kill a man." I wasn't dead but I did get a pretty good jolt. It knocked me flat but I got right up and stayed in the game. Another time, at home, I knocked myself out going after a long fly ball. I rammed full speed into the left-field fence. But I walked away from that one, too.

The only other time I was hurt that year came the night a fast ball smashed me over the left eye. They said that you could hear the crack all over the park. White ran out to me. Again, I think he thought I was dead. When I woke up, seeing stars, I said, "It's lucky it hit me in the head." They took me to the hospital for observation. It was my first overnight stay in a hospital and I found I didn't like hospitals. I was out the next day ready to play, but they wouldn't let me.

Some people began to get the idea that I was fragile. Part of it was the all-out way I played; part of it was that I looked fragile. I weighed about 170 or 175. I was still a tall, skinny beanpole. People looked at my legs and began calling me "Pencils" and wondered how I could cut it with such skinny legs. The truth is, I was better off. I feel that the guy with thick legs is subject to muscle pulls and torn hamstrings and things like that. I never had any trouble of that kind, and I think it was because of my funny legs.

Another thing people were trying to figure out was where I got my power. Lots of times they'd look at me and say, "How can you hit the ball that far?" Well, I think you can be a 270-pounder and still not be able to hit the ball a long way. I think in baseball most of your power comes from your arms and your wrists and the strength of your back muscles. I think you're able to swing the bat quicker and faster if you've got the strength in your arms and wrists, and that's where the power comes, from the quickness of the bat and the grip that you have on the bat.

I had the strength then and the natural ability, but I wasn't consistent. I was still having trouble with the curve ball. I'd see the pitcher wind up and that's what I would see. Period. In 1954 I hit twenty-five home runs with a month to go in the season and I didn't hit another home run. Part of it was that I was tired. I still suffered off and on from stomach trouble and those Sunday games, played in a hot sun at 105, 106 degrees, weakened me. But mostly, I wasn't following the ball.

Still, it was a good season all-around. I remember we were battling Jacksonville for the pennant and in one game against them I hit a home run and we won it, 2–1. I ended with a batting average of .336, 110 runs batted in, and a league-leading 112 runs scored. And Gabe Paul called me right after the season with good news. He said, "How would you like to train with the big club?"

I was elated. I said, "I'd love to."

So that was it. I felt I had a good chance to make the Reds in 1955. If I could have looked ahead a few months, even a few weeks, I would have had quite a different thought. I would have thought: Will I ever play baseball again?

6   A Close Call

The trouble started late in the 1954 season. I was trying to throw a runner out at the plate and I felt a sudden, sharp pain in my right shoulder. It was like I had been jabbed with a pin.

"You're probably just tired," Ernie White said. "It'll go away."

I didn't think much about it then. The Reds had decided to speed up my development by having me play winter ball in Puerto Rico and I was looking forward to it. I went down to Ponce and got off to a good start. I was hitting well and fielding well.

One night we were playing the San Juan team. It was a chill, raw night. In the eighth inning, we were two runs behind. I came up against Ruben Gomez, who was then with the New York Giants. There were two men on base and I caught hold of a fast ball and hit one of the longest home runs ever hit in that park.

In the ninth inning, our pitcher got in trouble and they pushed a man to third base. The next batter hit a long fly to right field. I drifted back, made the catch, and cut loose a throw to the plate, and the catcher put the tag on the runner trying to score.

I didn't see the end of that play. Making the throw, I had popped something in my right shoulder. It felt like springs had unwound in the shoulder and the pain was terrible, like the stab of a knife.

I walked off the field, my arm hanging loosely by my side.

The next day the arm was swollen to twice its size and it ached and felt numb. The Ponce general manager became

alarmed. He called Gabe Paul and the Reds made arrange-
ments for me to go to Cincinnati to have the arm examined.

I flew into Miami and the airline people told me they didn't
have a flight to Cincinnati. I asked them if they had a flight
to California. They did so I went home.

The next day the phone rang. It was Gabe Paul. "Where
the hell are you?" he asked.

"I'm home, in California," I said, as though this would be
a revelation to Paul. I told him about the plane reservation
and he was pretty mad about it. He told me to get to Cincinnati as soon as I could. But first I went to the University
of California to have a specialist examine the arm. The doctor
said I had a bone spur that was as big as the top of a little
finger. He said that unless it came out I would never be able
to throw again. I called Cincinnati and Gabe Paul almost
died when he heard the news. He told me to get to Cincinnati right away and have the doctor there examine it.

The doctor in Cincinnati couldn't find any bone spur. In
fact he couldn't find anything really wrong with the arm. He
just prescribed rest.

So I went back home and took it easy and waited for spring
training.

When I reported to the Reds at Tampa in the spring of '55,
I was surprised by the propaganda manager Birdie Tebbetts
was handing out to the newspapermen about me. "I was ready
to startle everybody," Birdie told a writer later, "by starting a
nineteen-year-old kid in the Cincinnati outfield. He was such
a great-looking young hitter, I was sure he could make it."

At that time, though, I didn't think I could make batboy
on the McClymonds High team. I honestly had visions of my
career being finished. I simply couldn't throw. They tried to
get me to throw the soreness out. That became the routine
each day. I would go with the B squad in the morning, then
always be dressed for the A game in the afternoon. Each day
was the same—throwing, throwing, throwing. Only it pained
me even to lob the ball.

Finally, with about two weeks left in spring training, the A team was at Clearwater to play the Phillies. I was with them and went down the sidelines, throwing lightly with an easy motion, a fluid motion. All of a sudden, my arm popped again and began to pain me like a toothache. The pain was more severe than I had ever experienced in my life. I thought I was going to pass out.

I put my jacket on and rode the bus back to Tampa where our trainer, Wayne Anderson, was going to give my shoulder a heat treatment. In the dressing room I removed my jacket and Anderson took one look at the arm and blanched. It had blown up the size of a watermelon and was all black-and-blue, where blood vessels had apparently broken. He left me and went into the office. He must have told them that something was really wrong because Gabe Paul came rushing into the trainer's room and said, "We're sending you to Cincinnati to have the arm examined."

Here we go again, I thought, another exercise in futility. I stayed in the Cincinnati hospital a few days while they took all sorts of tests; and, again, the doctors could find nothing. I must have seen twelve doctors in all, and no two had the same diagnosis. One said it was a bone spur, another said it was a calcium deposit. Two doctors advised an operation, but each doctor suggested a cut should be made in a different place.

Finally, I went to Johns Hopkins in Baltimore and was examined by Dr. George Bennett, a noted bone surgeon. He couldn't find anything wrong. He told me to be patient and that the arm would improve. That seemed to be the best advice of all and I went back to Cincinnati and they said, "We're sending you to Tulsa."

I told them, "Nope, I don't want to go back to Tulsa." I figured they didn't want me last year, why should I go with them now. Besides, the Reds only had a working agreement with Tulsa then—they weren't owned outright by the Reds

—and I didn't think Tulsa would have my best interests at heart. I told them I'd rather go back to Columbia.

And that's what I did and Ernie White said he was glad to have me. White was a fiery type of leader who hated to lose, but he was very patient with me. He played me at first base so I wouldn't have to make any long throws.

It was rough at the beginning. I couldn't throw a ball ten feet without the arm swelling from the shoulder down to the wrist. First base was all right but I couldn't even roll the ball around the infield. One day there was a runner on third with less than two out. The batter hit the ball back to the mound. The runner on third waited until the pitcher threw to first, then he broke for the plate. I hopped the ball home, screaming as I threw because the pain was so bad. I was really scared.

For three months I was in and out of the hospital at Columbia. My arm would swell up and I would go to the hospital for heat treatments, play a couple of weeks, then go back to the hospital. I wasn't helping the club much and I wasn't helping myself. My hitting had fallen off next to nothing. At one time, my batting average was .190, and the fans, even the home fans, began to get on me.

One night it all came to a head. We were playing at home, and I was playing first base and three drunken guys sitting in the stands began to get on me. I mean, get on me. The ball park at Columbia wasn't too big, the seats maybe twenty-five feet from the playing field, and I heard everything.

As the game wore on it got worse and worse. They became vicious with racial remarks and the language thrown in. It was very personal and very abusive and—I don't care who it is, a ballplayer or anyone—nobody should have to take that kind of stuff.

It was the ninth inning and we were losing the ball game, anyway, and I was on first base after getting a hit. There were two outs and the next batter hit a fly ball to the outfield and the outfielder caught the ball for the third out, ending the game. I ran the ball out, then came back to the dugout, grabbed a bat, and started after the three guys. I got inside the fence leading to the temporary stands and went up after them.

Marv Williams, my teammate and a good friend, grabbed me. He threw his arms around my chest, not letting me move. "It isn't worth it," he said. And, really, he was right, but he didn't seem right at the time.

Ernie White came running over. "What's wrong?" I told him and he said, "Tell me who they are, I'll get them for you."

White did get the license number of the automobile they drove off in. Later, he wrote the owner a letter. He told him that if he and his friends doubted Frank Robinson's courage, he would arrange a meeting for them with Robinson. They never answered.

But now I had had it. My career was at the crossroads. I was wondering if it would be cut short. I was more concerned than ever because my arm wasn't coming around. It was just ruining the whole season for me. I thought, is this really the end of my career? Will I ever come around again?

I had plenty of time to think, you know, living in Columbia and not being able to go where I wanted. I always liked to be around people and this was like a prison. I just couldn't sit and stare at the four walls in my room. I was very lonely, and bitter. I felt I was giving everything I had to give even though I was not in good physical shape, and I was not earning any respect in return. I was at a point where I couldn't take it any more.

The team was leaving for a ball game in Charlotte, North Carolina, ninety miles away, and I told my roomie, Marv Williams, who was the only other Negro on the club, "I might as well go home."

Marv said, "If you're not going to Charlotte, I'm not going."

I went and told Bill McCarthy, the general manager. I said, "I'm through. I'm going home."

He tried to talk me out of it. "It's a mistake, Frank. Stick it out, go with the team. It's got to get better, you'll see."

I wasn't convinced. "No," I said, "I've had it."

Bill said, "Why don't you at least give me a day or so to talk to Gabe Paul and see what he has to say and what he wants me to do."

I said, "You can call, but I don't guarantee that I'll be around."

The next day the team took off on the bus and Marv and I stayed behind.

What happened then was like an act of Providence. The game that night at Charlotte was rained out. That gave me time to think more about what I had done. And it began to dawn on me that I was throwing away any chance I had to become a major-leaguer, that I was throwing away my whole life. I thought, what the heck, who am I hurting but myself?

I told Marv, "I've changed my mind. Let's go back." He said okay and a friend of ours drove us to Charlotte and we didn't miss the game. We played a doubleheader that night and I started to hit better.

A few days later back in Columbia, my arm still hurting, I made another decision. I just said to myself, "The heck with it, I'm not going to throw a baseball for two weeks." And I didn't. I didn't touch a baseball in that time. Then I started to throw easy on the sidelines and the arm began to come back. One day late in the season I was able to cut loose from the outfield and throw out a runner trying to score. I knew then my arm was sound again.

Suddenly, everything began to fall in place. The team began to gather momentum. We were eight games behind Jacksonville at the time but we really began to move. We won thirty-eight of our last forty-two games and won the Sally League pennant. In the last six weeks of the season I

[1] Members of McClymonds' championship basketball team, 1950-51. I'm up top next to coach George Powles, a man who had a tremendous influence on my life. One important player is missing from this shot: Bill Russell.

[2] I was a third baseman in high school (second from the left, *not* the boy with the toothpick). You couldn't play the outfield in high school. That wasn't the glamorous position.

[3] Frank Robinson in 1956, a rookie in major-league baseball. It was a good year. I batted .290, hit thirty-eight homers, and was named National League Rookie of the Year. (Photograph by UPI.)

[4] My best friend in baseball was, and still is, Vada Pinson. We roomed together for six years on the Reds. We spoke the same language, and he liked to do the things I liked to do—taking in movies, watching TV, just sleeping. (Photograph by *Sport Magazine*.)

batted .390 and hit ten of my twelve home runs for the year. I ended with a .263 average, but that didn't bother me at all. I felt I still had a future in this game of baseball. That was all that mattered.

7 Rookie

Sometime in the winter of 1956 I received a letter from the Reds inviting me to train with them again, and I was very happy about that. All I wanted was the opportunity to make the team and the Reds had given it to me in 1955, and now they were giving me another chance.

We all have a tendency, I think, to look back on our lives at something bad that happened to us and say—from the sanctuary of the years—"it was a blessing in disguise." Looking back at that 1955 season, at the sore arm, at all my frustrations as a ballplayer and as a human being, my inclination is to say, "It was a blessing in disguise."

I had hit very well in spring training of '55 and if I hadn't had the arm trouble, I probably would have gone up to the big club. But I think I might have failed. I don't think I was ready for the major leagues in 1955 and, had I failed, I think it would have had a deep emotional effect on me.

Looking back (again, the years tend to soften one's sour experiences) I would say I needed that second year at Columbia. I would say that it did me much good. Although I didn't perform very well, I still learned quite a bit down there about myself as an athlete—what I could do and what I couldn't do—and as a person.

I began to mature a bit. I learned not to let things get under my skin quite as much, not to let petty annoyances bother me as much. I was still a loner and just unable to unburden myself, talk things out, with higher authorities or the players I was friendly with. I still kept too much to myself, but I think the beating I took from the fans down south for most of that year did help mature me.

But mostly I learned more about being a ballplayer. On the field, I was able to experiment because I wasn't hitting, anyway. I was able to try things. I tried to hit the ball to right field, to go with the pitch a little more. And I was able to follow the ball better.

A fellow who had a great influence on me that year was Marv Williams. He had been around in the minor leagues for a long time and he knew quite a bit about baseball and he talked a lot of baseball to me. He helped my performance on the field and if I hadn't been at Columbia in 1955 and seen Marv, I might never have come up with the stance I used for nine years in the major leagues, with the bat hung over my shoulder almost parallel to the ground.

That's the way Marv batted. He laid the bat back over his shoulder and he hit line drives all over the place. About the only guy I ever remember seeing who batted like that was Gil McDougald of the Yankees, but he laid the bat down, he didn't get it back on his shoulder. So I started to bat like Marv that year at Columbia, when I was commuting from the hospital. I laid my bat parallel to the ground and started hitting the ball.

But when I reported to the Reds at Tampa in late February of 1956, I felt that still wasn't enough. I had thought a lot about it. In the minors I stood deep in the box and away from the plate, and that worked well enough against minor-league pitching. Coming into the major leagues would be a different matter. I would be up against pitchers who were much smarter than me, who had been around a long time, who had much more experience, and better control, especially on their breaking pitches. I asked myself, what am I going to do to neutralize the experience the pitchers have over me? What can I do? I just sat down and thought it out, and came up with a plan.

I decided to move up on the plate. Pitchers like to have the whole plate to work with—to come in on you and then go away from you. I decided I wouldn't give them the complete plate to shoot at. I felt if I gave them the inside of the plate (at least until I got two strikes on me) and protected the outside corner, I would be better off. I wasn't the type of hitter to hit the outside pitch off balance to right field, back off the plate. I felt if I was up on the plate, I'd be able to handle the outside pitch and pull it to a certain degree if I wanted to, or I could go to right field just by not swinging or turning my wrist over as much as I would have if I was trying to pull the ball.

That was my thinking and I tried it. I stood about even with home plate with my feet up against the chalk line in front of the batter's box, bent slightly from the waist, hanging my head in what they call "concussion alley," so I could get a good look at the pitch.

And, right away that spring, I began to hit the ball good.

I didn't get into the lineup immediately because my arm was sore and manager Birdie Tebbetts didn't want me in there, possibly cutting loose with a throw. I worked the soreness out gradually and stayed on the bench during the early intraquad games.

My first time at bat in one of those games, I went up to pinch-hit against Joe Black. I squeezed in there, hanging tight over the plate, my bat held back on my shoulder, feeling real comfortable with that new stance.

On the first pitch Black fed me a fast ball and I swung and hit the ball on a line 390 feet over the right-center-field fence.

It was a good start and it made me feel that I might belong with this ball club.

All spring I hit well. In twenty-seven exhibition games, my batting average was .271, with fourteen runs batted in, twenty-two runs scored, and four home runs. I was encouraged but I still had no assurance that I was going to make the squad. I was a non-roster player then, up for a look, and trying to crash a lineup packed with power hitters. The Reds had Ted Kluszewski, Gus Bell, Wally Post, Ray Jablonski, Smoky

Burgess, and Bob Thurman. In 1955 Post, the right fielder, hit forty home runs; Kluszewski hit forty-seven; Bell, twenty-seven; Burgess, twenty-one. I figured I did have two advantages: 1. the Reds did not have a left fielder, and 2. they were looking for a right-handed-hitting power hitter. Klu, Bell, and Burgess were left-handed, and if I could make the team, Birdie would have a better-balanced lineup.

When I reported to the Reds that March, Birdie told me I would make the team if my arm came around, and all spring he did everything he could to help me. Unlike 1955 when I was billed as the Second Coming, Tebbetts played down my reputation. He told writers that his goal for Frank Robinson was a .265 batting average and fifteen home runs. Well, I personally thought that was kind of low, but I didn't say anything because that kind of talk helped keep me loose.

The arm loosened up, too. On April 12 we were playing an exhibition game with the Senators in Chattanooga, Tennessee. I was in the outfield before the game shagging flies when Gabe Paul, who was sitting in the stands, called me over. I walked over slowly, thinking he was going to tell me that he was sending me out.

He said, "Frank, you've had a fine spring. We're adding you to the roster."

I celebrated by hitting a home run against the Senators.

On April 17 I was in the starting lineup for the traditional Monday Opening Day in Cincinnati.

And I still remember that day like it was yesterday.

It was a raw, cloudy afternoon with the temperature in the forties. There was an overflow crowd at Crosley Field, some of the spectators spilling into the outfield. That meant that any ball hit into the crowd would be a ground-rule double and I remember asking myself what I was going to do if I had to go back for a long fly.

I also remember asking myself how I was going to handle the St. Louis Cardinals' pitcher, Vinegar Bend Mizell. He was a big, strong left-hander who had just come back to the

Cardinals after two years in the Army. His best pitch was his fast ball, but he had the usual major-league assortment.

I wasn't too worried about Mizell, though, partly because I liked fast-ball pitchers and partly because manager Birdie Tebbetts had me batting seventh in that opening-day lineup. This was the batting order:

Johnny Temple	2B
Smoky Burgess	C
Ted Kluszewski	1B
Wally Post	RF
Gus Bell	CF
Ray Jablonski	3B
Frank Robinson	LF
Roy McMillan	SS
Joe Nuxhall	P

Lots of big bats in that lineup, which made it easy for me to snuggle in without a fuss.

The game was scoreless going to the last of the second inning. Then Ray Jablonski came up and hit a home run.

The crowd was still buzzing about Jabbo's home run when I dug in the batter's box, awaiting the first pitch of my major-league career. Going unnoticed like that was fine with me; it made me feel nice and relaxed.

I don't think Mizell was too concerned about me, a rookie, in his first time at bat. Anyway, he didn't work on me too much. I guess he was going to try me out and see if I could hit a fast ball. He gave me the fast ball right down the middle. I liked this fast ball very much. I hit it off the center-field wall for a double, missing a home run by a couple of feet.

I wound up the day two for three—the double, a single, and an intentional walk. But we lost the game. It was 2–2 going to the ninth inning when Red Schoendienst scratched a single off Nuxhall, and Stan Musial came up and beat us with a home run.

I must admit, though, that I felt real good after the game. The writers came up to me in the dressing room and asked me what I thought of major-league pitching, and the way it came out in the papers next day, it sounded like I was a real hot dog.

"The pitching's pretty much the same as the Sally League," I was reported as saying. But that wasn't what I meant. I meant that basically there wasn't that much difference in the pitching, the *type* of pitching. You see some pitchers in the minors who are able to throw harder than some pitchers in the majors, but the pitchers in the major leagues are much smarter, much more seasoned, and are able to work the hitters a lot more than the young kids in the minor leagues.

I had that point driven home to me right away.

In the next five games on the road, I got two singles and a double in twenty-one times up, and I struck out six times. It was a horrible record and I think if I didn't have an understanding manager and an understanding front office, I might have been back in the minor leagues.

We came back home with a night game scheduled and Birdie Tebbetts came up to me and said, "You're not playing tonight."

I wasn't shocked; in fact, I kind of expected it. Birdie explained, "I've seen too many young kids get in a slump and keep playing and keep playing, and some of them have had their careers ruined that way. I'm going to sit you down tonight and tomorrow you'll be in the lineup."

And I did sit down that night, replaced by Stan Palys, and I did start the next afternoon against the Chicago Cubs. And I hit the first home run of my major-league career. It came in the second inning off Paul Minner and when I came back to the dugout all my teammates were up applauding. That was a real thrill for me, real warming, for big-league players to applaud a rookie hitting a home run. For it meant they had accepted me and were glad to have me on the ball club. It really made me feel good and made me relax a bit more. I had been a little tense and edgy up to then but now I felt I was home.

And I went on kind of a spree after that. The next day I hit my second home run. It bounced off the light tower in back of right-center field, high above the fence. A couple of days later I hit my third home run against Carl Erskine of the Dodgers, over the center-field fence. From April 28 to May 6, I hit five home runs.

Actually, I never really doubted that I could hit major-league pitching. I have never belittled a pitcher's ability, but no pitcher has ever awed me and I have always had confidence in my ability. And I always felt that I could hit in the major leagues, given the chance. And Birdie Tebbetts gave me that chance.

He sat me down only three times my rookie year. The first was when I was in that early-season slump. The next two came when two outstanding National League pitchers went up against us for the first time in 1956, Robin Roberts and Don Newcombe. Birdie said he wanted me to watch both men from the bench the first time, wanted me to study them, get an idea of how they threw, what they threw, the way they threw. The funny thing is, once I did get to bat against them I did very well, especially Newcombe. That was because Don's best pitch was a fast ball and his second-best pitch was a hard slider and he had no off-speed pitches.

But that was Birdie Tebbetts' way of educating me. He had left a deep impression on me ever since I first came in contact with him in 1955 in spring training. Birdie was not only a manager, he was like a father to me. He always took time with his ballplayers to explain things to them, tell them why he was doing things and why he wasn't, and why one ballplayer was playing today and another one wasn't playing. He was always explaining the inside of the game, the plays that were occurring on the field, as they happened.

If you were sitting on the bench he always wanted you near him, especially the young players. When a situation came up, he would always point it out to the young players, and he always kept the bench alive by walking up and down asking the players the count on the hitter, how many outs there were, things like that. He always tried to keep his players in the game.

Whatever alertness I have today, I owe to Birdie. In those early days of my baseball career he often took me aside and talked to me and gave me advice. He taught me to think ahead, to anticipate on the baseball field, to stay on top of things in the dugout between innings. I learned from Birdie that you can pick up a lot of things in that dugout—a pitcher throwing a certain way, one of your own teammates doing something wrong. That's why, to this day, I'm sitting in the dugout and I'm always watching and learning and trying to pick up something, either from my own teammates or the opposition.

If I made mistakes—and I made plenty that year—Birdie would take me aside and explain what I had done wrong. A couple of times no explanation was needed. One game I let Roy McMillan catch a fly ball in short left when I could have made the catch and thrown out the runner, who scored after McMillan's tough catch. Another day I missed third base going from second to home. Always, Birdie would take me aside and gently—for he is a gentle man—explain my mistakes.

I remember one game against the Philadelphia Phillies when we were down 3–2 in the eighth inning. I was on second base and Ed Bailey was up and I thought I could steal third. In this situation we were supposed to look in the dugout. Birdie would either give us the little shrug of the shoulder and say okay or shake his head yes or no. So, this day, I looked in the dugout and kept lookin' and lookin' . . . and nothin'. So I took off, and was thrown out.

I came back and Birdie said, "Why'd you do that?"

I said, "Well, I looked in the dugout and you weren't paying any attention to me."

He said, "Frank, I'm sorry about that, I really am, but it

doesn't matter if I give you the sign or not. Anytime you're on second base and you try to steal third, you shouldn't be thrown out. You don't go unless you can make it."

Well, I was twenty-one years old and still had plenty to learn.

One thing I had plenty to learn about was playing the outfield.

There was one game when I was a butcher out there. It was beautiful.

We were playing the Milwaukee Braves and Bill Bruton hit a line drive out to me, and I dropped it. I just didn't flip my glove out right. I had the glove sort of level with the ground and the palm was up and the ball just skipped through my hand and right on down and dropped on the ground. If I'd turned the glove around with the palm facing the infield, it would have been an easy catch.

Danny O'Connell hit a sinking line drive to left. I came hard to try and catch it. I thought I had a good chance, but when I got near the ball, I realized I couldn't catch it. Because of my inexperience I didn't stop and try to block the ball. I continued on and it got by me and rolled to the fence.

Finally, I made one good play. Frank Torre hit a pop fly to left and I came in fast and picked the ball off my shoe-tops. Only the umpire called it a trap. That just made the night complete.

The trouble with me was I just wasn't a real good out-fielder. I always had trouble out there on the movement and the turning required, and I had trouble going back on balls, especially on balls hit directly over my head. But Hal Jeffcoat, a spare outfielder with the Reds and a defensive specialist, worked with me each day hitting balls to me for ten or fifteen minutes. And he often sat down and talked to me and helped me in planning out things—what I should do or try to do in the outfield.

Crosley Field was a particular problem, especially for a young kid, because they had a terrace out there, an incline, that went up like a hill twenty-five feet from the wall. It just gradually went up to the wall and it was pretty difficult when you hit it. If you didn't hit it just right you'd fall flat on your face. And in those days Crosley Field had a brick wall and you'd go up for a fly ball or a line drive and if it hit the wall it would richochet off and then you'd have to chase it down from the hill.

But my play out there improved as the year went on. I've always profited by mistakes, and I was profiting heavily my rookie year. At least I knew I wasn't a polished outfielder and that I had to work a little harder and try to improve all the time. To this day I feel that way about my outfielding. I'm never satisfied with my performance and am still trying to improve.

I may have been second best in the outfield, but at least my manager knew I was trying harder. Five times in 1956 I crashed into fences going after fly balls. Each time I'd be knocked out or stunned, and Birdie would rush out to see if I was all right. He got kind of tired of that act so one day he said to me, "Look, Frank, the next time you hit a wall, I'm not going to leave the dugout. I'm getting too old to walk 450 feet for nothing."

Well, we were playing in Pittsburgh one day and I hit the fence in left-center trying to make the catch, and I held the ball and then fell to the grass, stunned.

The other outfielders ran over and they took one look at me with my eyes closed and they hollered for the trainer and a stretcher. This alarmed the manager and he picked himself up off the bench and walked out to see if I was all right.

I was still on the ground when Birdie got there, but by this time I had recovered my senses. He bent over me and I opened my eyes and said, "What took you so long?" Then I jumped up and walked away.

Actually, I only really hurt myself twice that year. I did get hit by pitches twenty times, which led the National League by a big margin, but none were very serious. Mostly, they were glancing blows or they would hit me in the back where it didn't hurt very much . . . since I had a little meat back there. It was annoying, but I didn't say too much. I left it up to the manager to make the statements, and sometimes he got very mad about the treatment he felt I was receiving. But to me, I think it was a case of the pitchers trying to intimidate me, or get me mad, or move me back off the plate.

A lot of times the pitchers claimed my arm was in the strike zone; they said I was hit by strikes. I didn't pay any attention to that either because I didn't know if the pitch that hit me was a strike or not. Some of them were close, I'll admit that. They could have been strikes if they hadn't hit me, but that's the way it was.

On June 25 we were playing the Pittsburgh Pirates. There were two outs in the second inning and I was on third base, and I decided to steal home.

I went in head-first and Pirate catcher Danny Kravitz came down on my arm trying to tag me and plate umpire Lee Ballanfant called me out. I was mad. I insisted that Kravitz had stepped on my arm to tag me after my outstretched hand had reached the plate. I offered proof—four dripping spike cuts on my right arm. But Ballanfant, true to the code, was unmoved by the sight of blood.

Our trainer, Wayne Anderson, applied first aid and I stayed in the game. In the seventh inning, Kluszewski homered and I singled and I scored the winning run on a single by Ed Bailey and a sacrifice fly to Jablonski.

Actually, they probably should have sewn the thing up. At the time it seemed more like a scrape than a deep cut, so they just wrapped it up and I kept playing. But after the All-Star game break it started opening pretty good and it bothered me for quite a while.

My other injury came late in the season after I hit my thirty-eighth home run, and it was especially frustrating. I had the knack then (I still do) of being able to check my swing in midstream. In those days some of the writers were comparing me to Ted Williams and Stan Musial, both of whom could stop their swings at the split second. With me it was a matter of good reflexes plus the strength in my wrists. I had always been able to start my swing and be able to stop it if it was a bad pitch. This was something new to the umpires and, at first, they used to call quite a few strikes on me on the half swing. They weren't used to it and I guess they just watched the bat when it started to go and they'd say, well, he swung. So I had quite a bit of trouble the first couple of months.

It got so that when Birdie Tebbetts went over the ground rules before the game, he would tell the umpire about my swing. He also ran a campaign in the papers and I think the umpires gradually became aware of it and started to be a little bit more consistent on their calls.

Anyway, we were playing in St. Louis with two weeks to go in the season and I sprained my wrist on a checked swing. I missed two games and it bothered me the rest of the way and I didn't hit one more home run. As a matter of fact, I didn't even come close. I just didn't have the snap in my bat any more. I'd just go up and try to hit the ball and place it, but I couldn't take my full swing.

The reason this was so frustrating was because I had tied Wally Berger's National League record for home runs by a rookie and I really wanted to break it, and I couldn't. To this day we share that record.

That was a disappointment, but other things made up for it. By the first week of July I was hitting .316, with eighteen home runs, and the fans voted me on the National League All-Star team. I became the youngest starter in an All-Star game and it was a tremendous thrill to be there, to play with people like Willie Mays, and to watch Ted Williams and fellows you'd always heard so much about.

As for the game itself . . . nothing. I got up twice against Billy Pierce. He threw a fast ball that tailed away and he struck me out twice on six pitches. He didn't waste a pitch.

After the All-Star break I was looking for fast balls that tailed away, or fast balls that came in, but I didn't see any. I didn't get to see many fast balls the rest of the season. In August I went into a slump and one enemy pitcher explained it to a newspaperman. "Robinson," this pitcher said, "doesn't like curve balls and we've quit throwing him fast balls."

That's exactly what was happening and they almost curved me out of the league. It was nothing but curve ball, curve ball, curve ball. I was seeing them in my sleep. But, looking back, I can see where the enforced diet of curves helped advance my career.

Curve balls are slow stuff and if a hitter sees enough of them, he can hit them. On the other hand, if a hitter can't handle a fast ball, he can never learn to. I could always handle the fast ball, but on the breaking ball I had to learn to stand back, not start my swing too soon. And I did, and I started hitting the curve ball better.

The night of my twenty-first birthday, August 31, we were playing the Cubs and I said I was going to try to give myself a present by hitting a home run. Bob Rush was beating us 3–2 and I led off the ninth and hit the home run, and we went on to win the game.

The only other time that season when I deliberately went after a homer came on September 4 against the Braves. It was the tenth inning, 2–2, and Ernie Johnson was the pitcher. I went up, hoping to break up the game. And I did.

We had a tremendous hitting team in 1956 and the real frustration of the season was not winning the pennant after being so close. As a team, we hit 221 home runs, which tied the National League record. But I'm sure we would have all sacrificed that for a pennant. As it was, we were in the pennant race until the last week of the season, and then we wound up third. It was a real disappointment in what otherwise was a fine season for me.

I ended up with a batting average of .290, and I led the league in runs scored with 122. I drove in eighty-three runs and I felt that was quite an accomplishment because I started the season hitting sixth and seventh and then, after a few months, I started hitting second after Johnny Temple. Someone figured out that in 1956 Mickey Mantle and myself led the majors in driving in the winning run—eight games. I drove in the winning run once with a sacrifice fly, three times with singles, and four times with home runs.

When I was the unanimous choice as National League Rookie of the Year, that kind of capped it all for me. I felt very pleased about that. Nobody could have asked for more out of his rookie year and I should have been as happy as a kid opening birthday presents.

But I wasn't. My rookie year hadn't been that easy for me, certainly not as easy as it looked in the statistics. There were things that bothered me all season long, and were to continue to bother me in my early years in the major leagues.

Gabe Paul said it: "Frank was like a lost soul then. He had no companionship. When you're young your mind is full of problems, whether imaginary or real. Frank felt he had problems and he didn't know how to work them out."

They weren't big problems. I can't even remember half of them today. And maybe if I'd gone and talked them over with someone else, I might have worked them out quicker. But that wasn't my way. I had to hold them in and try to work them out myself. That was just my way of doing things.

The main reason I kept things to myself was that I had a feeling of not belonging. As well as I did in 1956, at no time that year did I feel I was a real part of the team. I did my job on the baseball field and that's where it ended, when I left the baseball field.

One thing was that there was no one my age on the ball club. I was the youngest and since I was a loner anyway, a fellow who doesn't make friends easy, it was doubly hard to be twenty-one years old playing on a team with fellows five or ten years older. I did my job and everyone was nice to me but when the game was over they went their way and I went my own way.

I lived at the Manse Hotel in Cincinnati, which was a hotel for Negroes. All the Negro players on the Reds stayed there—Brooks Lawrence, George Crowe, Bob Thurman, and Pat Scantlebury. Because we were Negroes we did have mutual interests but these were all older fellows and I just never felt that I belonged. I was never able to sit down and talk baseball with them and my ideas were so different, so completely different, because they were much older than me.

I used to tag along with Brooks Lawrence and Bob Thurman after the game, not because it was fun but because I didn't have anything else to do. They liked to go to nightclubs, and I just wasn't in with that type of a crowd and I didn't drink. I just sat there in a corner in a booth looking at my watch and hoping they would get tired and we could go back to the hotel.

What I liked to do—and nobody else seemed to like—was go to three or four movies a day. I would do this especially when we were on the road and we pulled a night game. I would get up in the morning and have breakfast and go to the movies. I'd get out of one movie and go see another one, and that sort of filled up my time until it was time to go to the ball park.

Otherwise, I stayed in my room and wrote letters. I wrote a lot of letters. I wrote home quite often. Since I didn't have anyone to talk to, I felt better when I wrote, especially someone who was close to me. And it always gave me something to do.

There was another thing, too, another thing that I learned in 1956, like a kid who finally pulls his head out of the stars. I realized for the first time that baseball wasn't really fun any more.

I don't mean that I didn't love the game; it wasn't that. I still went out there with great anticipation, I still looked forward to playing each game. But now it was more of a job than a game. It was a job because the fun and laughter, the excitement, the carefree air, the easygoing atmosphere was gone. You see, I'd always been a carefree, easygoing guy, and that's the way baseball had been to me. In high school, sand-lot ball, American Legion, the minor leagues . . . baseball had always been fun. At Ogden we won the pennant by something like thirteen games and I had a good year and the team had a good year and it was still fun. The following year at Columbia it was the same, even though I was playing in the South and the team finished fourth, which I wasn't too happy about. But I had a good year, and it was still fun. My last year in Columbia, when I was hurt and when the fans got on me wasn't very much fun, I'll admit that, but it came back near the end when we won the pennant and my arm came around. And I thought it would be the same way in the majors.

There were some things I just didn't realize. The pressures weren't so fierce playing in the minors. And I was around more with men my age, mostly working their way up. No one was making too much money in the minor leagues, especially in the lower classifications, and baseball wasn't a life-or-death proposition.

Then when I came up to the big leagues, there was more money involved. I made six thousand dollars my rookie year, which seemed like a small fortune to me at the time. There was more of everything involved. You knew, you knew in your heart, that this was it. That there was no place to go from here but down. This was what you had been working toward, and now you were here. Now you were around a different age group. You were around guys from twenty to forty, all on the top rung and trying to hang on. Suddenly, you were thrust into the arena with the lions, in the fiercest competition of our competitive society.

I called that period "the dark side of baseball" for me. Still, I'm sure I brought it on myself. My teammates were friendly to me, the people in Cincinnati were friendly to me.

It was my fault that I didn't go out and meet people. I was in a shell, and it would take some years before I came out.

But at least I had proved myself as a ballplayer that rookie year of 1956. I had done that all right. I was twenty-one years old and I knew I belonged in the major leagues and that was a comforting thought. Another was, I knew it had to get better as I grew up a little more.

8 How I Won My Fight with Fear

My second year in the majors, 1957, is one that really gets away from me. I do remember that when I was in spring training, everybody was talking about the sophomore jinx and asking me if I felt it would affect me. And I told them I didn't think there was any such thing as a sophomore jinx. And I think that's the year I proved that.

But maybe the sophomore jinx struck me in my third year, 1958. Maybe it was a delayed-action thing. Because 1958 was a horrible year for me. It was the year I was almost driven out of the major leagues. It was the year I waged a long, lonely fight with fear.

There were no such intimations as I prepared for the '57 season. I spent part of my first winter as a major-leaguer in Cincinnati, attending Xavier University.

That was Gabe Paul's idea. He talked to me about it and said the ball club would pay all my college expenses—tuition, books, and things. So I tried it. That's what it really was, a trial period more than anything else. But I had been away from school too long, too long away from books, from the routine of going to class and studying. I just couldn't get back to it. I pulled out after a month or so.

I think what Gabe Paul had in mind was that school would help me mature faster, would help me out of my shell. What Gabe Paul didn't understand—and maybe I didn't myself— was that the shell around me was really part of me. That was my makeup, my personality. I didn't make friends that easy. I didn't talk an awful lot. That's just the way I was. It kind of frightened me to meet people, to go out and see people I didn't know. So I just stayed around a small group, the people I knew.

But that winter in Cincinnati did help me. I came to meet more people my age, and because we had mutual interests, I was able to associate with them more off the field. We talked about the same things and they understood my problems and we were able to communicate better.

On the field that season of 1957 there were very few personal problems, although it was a disappointing year for the Cincinnati ball club. We started off very fast and at one point won twelve games in a row. We were in first place for about a month but after the All-Star break our pitching fell apart and we finished fourth. Brooks Lawrence was our best pitcher with a 16–13 record, and George Crowe was our big power hitter with thirty-one homers and ninety-two runs batted in.

I had a real good year, too. My home run output dropped from thirty-eight to twenty-nine, but that didn't alarm me. I didn't expect to come in again with thirty-nine or forty home runs. I only drove in seventy-five runs and I was a little disappointed about that, but that was mostly because I hit second all year long. I did raise my batting average from .290 to .322, with 197 hits.

I tied for third in the National League in hitting with Hank Aaron and I was very pleased that I had brought my average up thirty-two points. That's quite a jump anytime, especially for a second-year man.

I don't think there's any one explanation for my improvement as a hitter. It was a combination of things. Part of it, I'm sure, was because I was learning more about batting. After seeing so many curve balls I began to hit them a little better. I was probably a little bit smarter in certain situations, too. I was learning the pitchers and how they were trying to work me—what pitches they were throwing me, how they were trying to get me out in certain situations, and the pitches they were having the best luck with in getting me out. I kept a mental book in my head on things like that.

I had no unique theories about batting then, and I don't now. In those days, I used all kinds of bats. I broke in with a big, thick-barreled bat with a thick handle. It was thirty-five inches long and thirty-five ounces and I choked up on it. I soon discarded it because it was too much bat, too heavy for me to swing. I started using different bats of my own, then I started picking up other players' bats. I didn't order too many bats in those days because every time I found a bat I liked and would order a load, I would stop getting hits with it. So I just began using the other players' bats, and I told them when they ordered theirs, to order an extra dozen for me with their names on it.

I'm not that erratic now. My routine is to start off in spring training and the early part of the year (when I feel a little stronger) with a thirty-five-ounce bat. But as the season wears on, I usually drop down an ounce at a time. And I generally wind up the season with a thirty-three-ounce bat.

In my early years I choked up on the bat. When I came in as a rookie, my idea was to choke up because I felt I would have better control of the bat and I would still be able to hit those long balls. And I did, so I continued to choke up on the bat for quite a few years. I've gotten away from it now.

All this worked for me but I don't suggest that what works for me will work for everyone. Every hitter has to find a stance that works for him, not because Ted Williams or Joe DiMaggio hit that way, or because Frank Robinson had a good year. The worst thing a hitter can do, I think, is imitate another hitter. A hitter has to find his own style, has to know what he can do with certain pitches. Above all, a hitter has to believe in himself.

There are certain elementary truths about hitting: You have to find a bat you can handle, you've got to keep the head still and watch the ball at all times. You have to watch the pitcher when he gets the sign—where his hand is, where the

ball is, and know, each time, where he releases the ball.
Things like that you have to know . . . then, in the words of
the poet, just get you a bat and go up there and swing.

And that's what I did all my sophomore year. And I had
good luck. And there were maybe two things that year that
stood out and that had some significance as I look back now.

One was a baserunning incident involving Johnny Logan
of the Milwaukee Braves.

The other was when I was hit on the head by Ruben
Gomez of the New York Giants.

The Milwaukee Braves in 1957 were the big team in the
National League, and they did a job on us. We couldn't seem
to beat them; I think we lost more one-run games to them
that year than to all the other teams put together.

It was a spirited rivalry between us because for quite a
while that year we were fighting them for the pennant. And
we went all-out against the Braves.

The Logan thing happened on a double-play situation.
Johnny was the shortstop and I was on first base. The ball
was hit to the second baseman, who flipped to Logan for the
force, and I went after him to break up the double play.
Understand, I didn't go out of the baseline. If you go out of
the baseline, you're automatically out. I've never been called
out for sliding outside the baseline. I just went after him
to break up the double play.

He was coming across the bag when I hit him. I cut him
pretty good on the shin, and he had to leave the game and
was out of action for six weeks.

There was nothing said about the incident at the time,
mind you. But the Logan spiking was the first in a series of
basepath collisions involving me over the years that built up,
one by one, to the point where I would get a reputation as a
man who cut down infielders.

Well, that's all right with me. My creed in baseball (as I've
tried to indicate) is to play all-out, always to go all-out, because that's the only way to play baseball. The possibility

of the infielder being wounded by spikes is part of baseball. That's the hazard of playing the infield. You can't get cut in the outfield because you don't come in contact with runners—you only come in contact with brick walls.

You also, if you are Frank Robinson, occasionally come in contact with pitched balls.

It's funny. I was hit twenty times in the National League my rookie year, far and away the leader in that dubious category. But I never got hurt. The reason I never got hurt was I was always able to pull my head out of the way in time. But on July 16, 1957, I wasn't quite quick enough.

Ruben Gomez was the pitcher in this game against the Giants. And Gomez had sort of a history of throwing at hitters. One of the classic baseball pictures of all time shows big, burly Joe Adcock, a bat in his hand, stalking Gomez, who has just thrown at Adcock. The fear in Gomez' face is not easily forgotten.

Adcock never caught up with Gomez, and Ruben was emboldened to keep up his head-hunting.

My first time up against Gomez I tripled. My second time up, I doubled. My third time up, on the first pitch, he hit me.

Was it deliberate? Well, it was a fast ball, *behind me,* and I just wasn't able to go back. If I'd gone back it probably would have hit me in the face.

As it was, it went crashing against the left side of my head and it cracked the spun-glass helmet I was wearing. It also knocked me flat.

I was carried off in a stretcher, put in an ambulance, and rushed to the hospital. Throughout, I never lost consciousness. I was very much aware of a large ache in the head, and a small fear in the heart.

The fear grew as they X-rayed me. I was very scared because of the possibility of a fractured skull. Thankfully, the X-rays were negative. I left the hospital the next morning and I played in the afternoon game.

I wasn't as mad about the beaning as was Birdie Tebbetts.

He thought I had been seriously hurt and he was concerned about my welfare and he told a sportswriter that I was being thrown at because I was a Negro and wouldn't talk back. "You don't see pitchers throwing at Ted Kluszewski, Stan Musial, Duke Snider," Birdie said.

But I couldn't buy that, and I can't today. As I said earlier, those guys were trying to test me. They were trying to see what I was made of. And the reason I didn't talk back was because I never did talk too much, I never did have too much to say on or off the field. It had nothing to do with what color I was.

I picked up the pieces after the beaning and if there was fear still left in me, it was just a residue, a small, out-of-the-way pocket somewhere in my being.

Despite Ruben Gomez, I went on and had the good season and I was voted National League Sophomore of the Year.

Then I joined the Marines.

It came about this way. I wanted to hook up in a six-month deal because I was getting near the draft age. I felt it would be better to enlist in the reserves, serve my six months of active duty, and then be put on the reserve list. It was the best possible world for the professional ballplayer because it meant he wouldn't lose much, if any, playing time.

I took the Air Force test first and they said the results wouldn't be back for two to three weeks. I told them I couldn't wait that long to get into the service—I wanted to be out for part of spring training at least. So I went down to Parris Island in South Carolina and took the Marine test. Two days later I was in the Marines.

At the time I took my physical they asked me if I had any old injuries. I told them about my shoulder, but that was the end of that. I went in and trained like everybody else, and at first, everything went along fine.

We had to go over the obstacle course every day and in the early days of training there was no problem. But after I'd been there a while, I began to have trouble jumping on the chin bar and pulling myself over. I didn't seem to have any strength in my right arm. It got worse, to a point where I could barely pull myself over the first obstacle.

But I didn't say anything about it. I was squad leader, and I couldn't complain. Other guys were having their troubles running the obstacle course in the required five minutes, and I was trying to help them out.

One day I was told to go over to the Navy Medical Center for an examination. They had found out about my shoulder and wanted to X-ray it.

The doc looked at the X-rays, looked at me, looked back at the X-rays, looked at me again. I got the idea that he was trying to tell me something.

Finally, he said, "What kind of work do you do?"

I said, "I'm a professional baseball player."

"Are you making pretty good money?"

I said yes.

"Are you saving any of it?"

"Some," I said, which was a lie. In those days the money went out as fast as it came in.

He said, "Well, you better make it fast and save it, because any day your career may come to an end."

That really shook me. He asked me if I had ever dislocated my shoulder, and I told him no. Then he told me there was calcium in the shoulder, and a lot of other stuff floating around in there. I left that room in a pretty poor mood.

Two weeks later we went on a hike from our barracks to the rifle range. Just as I was unstrapping my gear at the range, someone drove up in a Jeep. Private Frank Robinson was told to fall out and report to headquarters.

When I got there a major was waiting. He wasted no words. He told me flat out that I was unfit for the Marines, that my shoulder would never hold up.

In two and a half days I was out of the Marines with an honorable discharge.

I know a lot of people said in jest at the time (I hope it

was in jest) that money talks, and that I was bought out of the Marine Corps. But that's how it really happened. And now I had a new worry when I joined the Reds in the spring of 1958, the worry whether my arm would hold up long enough for me to log a few more years as a major-leaguer.

Well, in the short run the arm held up all right. It was the head that gave me trouble.

If I was troubled that spring I managed to conceal it very well. A reporter asked me if I had set any goals for the 1958 season.

"Sure," I said. "I expect to hit about .340, drive home 125 runs, and hit forty home runs."

Right after that brave prediction, everything fell apart.

About a week before Opening Day, we were playing an exhibition game against the Washington Senators in Portsmouth, Ohio. The ball park was very small, a sandlot really, with a very low fence all the way around and no background at all for the batters.

Camilo Pascual was pitching for the Senators. At that time he was a youngster just coming into his strength. He threw directly overhead. He had a big, breaking curve ball and a wicked fast ball.

I came up against him in the first inning and he threw that fast ball and I never saw the ball from the time he let it go. Other fellows said later that the ball seemed to follow me, like it was drawn by a magnet.

It hit me in the head, under my protective helmet and just below the left ear. It was the hardest I've been hit in my life.

I just went down and I was out. All I remember, until I woke up in the hospital in Portsmouth, was something crashing into my head.

Vada Pinson later told me he had tried to walk out to see me but his legs wouldn't take him, that he thought I was dead. He said when he did get to me, my eyes were closed and I was moaning, and his first thoughts were, "Good gosh, this is a game that didn't mean anything."

When I came to in the hospital, they put me in an ambulance to take me back to Cincinnati, a 120-mile ride, and the road wasn't too good, and it didn't do my head any good.

I was very conscious and I felt every bump in the road. I didn't think I'd ever get to wherever it was they were taking me. They hadn't bothered to tell me anything and I didn't know where I was going. All I knew was that it was an awfully long ride. It seemed like fifteen hundred miles to me.

The worst thing was that I had all that time to think. Birdie Tebbetts had accompanied me to that Portsmouth hospital, along with Cincinnati newsmen. He was pretty frightened but he told the press, "This won't bother Robby. He's tough. He's been hit before. He won't scare."

But that wasn't what I was thinking on that long ride to the hospital in Cincinnati. I was thinking: Would this affect my hitting? Would I be plate shy, going away from the plate, or would I stand up at the plate the way I did before? I thought, could this be the end of my career? I just didn't know. The uncertainty of it all was what bugged me and that's what I kept thinking about all the time on that long ride to Cincinnati.

I spent three days in the hospital. X-rays were taken and they showed what was called a "cerebral concussion," but no fracture. Nothing was broken at least, and I was grateful for that.

The ball club swung up to the Washington-Baltimore area for exhibition games with those two ball clubs. The doctors had originally planned for me to stay in the hospital until the team returned to Cincinnati a day before Opening Day. But I didn't want to do that. I wanted to put myself to the test before Opening Day, before the season started. I wanted to have some questions answered, and I wanted them answered right away.

So I talked them into letting me go to Baltimore for the last two exhibition games. I went up there and Birdie was surprised but happy to see me.

I said, "I'm ready to play."

He said okay, but he didn't play me. He did let me pinch-hit in the game, however, and it didn't bother me.

The next day I did start the game only it didn't serve much of a purpose because the Orioles brought in a kid who was wilder than anybody I'd ever seen. And Birdie told all the players that if they stood too close to the plate to swing off that guy, he'd fine us. So that didn't prove anything to me.

And so I was going into the 1958 season with the questions unanswered. I was also going into the season with headaches and blurred vision, though I wouldn't admit it to the team or the team doctor.

The blurred vision bothered me a lot more than the headaches. The headaches were pretty constant, but mild. They were just aggravating. The blurred vision is what scared me. It wasn't too bad, I was able to see the ball good, but it did have me frightened.

The headaches went away after about a month and so did the blurred vision, but by that time it was too late. Maybe it would have all been different if I had followed the doctor's advice and not played until I was fully recovered. Maybe the fear would never have risen to the top. As it was, I went up there with my head throbbing, and that throbbing became a constant reminder of the beaning and the fact that it could happen again.

In that first month the fear was agonizing. I didn't feel it sitting on the bench waiting to hit, or stepping into the batter's box. It came on me subconsciously when the pitch was on its way to the plate. I'd flinch and roll back on my heels on the breaking balls. You can never hit a curve ball that way. You can roll back on a fast ball and still hit it because it comes in a straight line. But when you roll back on your heels with a curve ball, you have to reach for it.

And this continued after my headaches disappeared, and the pitchers knew what was happening and really gave it to me.

Normally, when you're hitting well, you might see six fast balls out of ten pitches. But when you're not hitting well, especially when you're not hitting the breaking ball, you'll see seven or eight breaking balls to two fast ones. And that's what was happening with me. They were throwing me curves that broke on the outside corner of the plate. I was rocking back and taking them for strikes. The more I took, the more I received.

I think pitchers talk a lot among themselves about certain things, especially about batters' weaknesses. Whitey Ford once wrote a magazine story called, I think, "The Great Pitchers' Union," how pitchers from other teams help each other by offering tips on a batter's latest weakness, or bad habit. And the word got out about me—Frank Robinson was falling away on breaking pitches.

Everyone was making excuses for me. "His stance is altered . . ." "He's gotten out of the groove . . ." My teammate Bob Thurman told a newspaperman, "He's been taking too many pitches. Now he can't make up his mind. His timing has been thrown off."

The excuses were offered, and so was the advice, and I had to do all kinds of experimenting in batting practice. After all, if the manager says something, you have to at least try it.

They had it figured out that I was striding too much, so they had me close up instead of taking the big stride. And they had me swinging, just trying to meet the ball. All kinds of things, all kinds of advice, the kind all ballplayers get when they're in a slump.

If it had been an ordinary slump, I still would maintain that the best thing to do is not listen to other people. I think a ballplayer, if he knows himself as a ballplayer and what he's able to do and what he isn't able to do, can sit down and talk to himself and work out the problem by himself. He's much better off doing that than sitting down and listening to a lot of advice. That's how a lot of ballplayers get fouled up, by listening to advice from different people who really don't know him. If you know yourself as a ball-player, and you're able to work these things out yourself, you're much better off. I think your slump won't persist as long.

But this was not an ordinary slump. Nobody knew what I was really experiencing. They may have seen me "pulling out" (that's what it's called, pulling out of the ball). They noticed that, yes, but they didn't know why. I was the only one who knew why and, true to my nature, I told no one.

At the All-Star break, my batting average was .240, I had eight home runs and twenty-three runs-batted-in . . . and the fear was still alive within me. There was some talk of sending me back to the minors, that I might have an easier time down there working out whatever demon was possessing me.

That three-day vacation at All-Star time gave me a chance to think hard about my problem. I said to myself, well, what are you going to do? Are you going to rebound from this thing or are you just gonna let 'em run you out of the major leagues and back to the minor leagues or maybe out of base-ball? I said, either you're gonna have to stand up at the plate and take your cuts and hit the curve ball or get run out of baseball.

The night before the season resumed we had an exhibition game scheduled in Seattle against our top minor-league team. I made up my mind that I was going to go back up there and start swinging the bat the way I used to. I resolved I was going to hit every ball to right field, no matter where it was pitched. When a right-handed hitter goes to right field, it means you have to stay in there longer than you would normally if you tried to pull the ball. This wasn't a league game so I wasn't reluctant to sacrifice myself and try to hit the ball into right field.

I got up four times in that game. Each time I hit the ball into right field. Twice I got base hits.

That game was really something I needed. It served a pur-pose. It built my confidence back up.

Our next game—and first regularly scheduled game since the All-Star break—was in San Francisco against the Giants. My family—my mother and two brothers—were at the game. That made me feel good, that bolstered my confidence.

In the second inning I went up to face Al Worthington. The score was 0–0. Worthington, a big right-hander, cranked and threw me a slow curve. And, this time, I didn't rock back on my heels. This time I stayed in there. This time I hit the curve good, hit it squarely, hit it over the left-field fence for a home run.

My next trip up I faced my old friend, Ruben Gomez. I drove in another run with a single, and we won the game, 4–0.

And, all of a sudden, the fear was gone.

The following day I hit a three-run home run off Marv Grissom in the eighth inning, and tied it in the ninth with a single. I went five for ten in that series—two home runs, five RBI.

The hitting continued. On July 17 at Wrigley Field my two-run homer helped us beat the Cubs, 3–2. The next day I hit one in the ninth and we beat the Cards, 2–1. Three days later we were in the bottom of the tenth losing 5–4. Gus Bell walked and I got up and homered over the left-field wall, and we won, 6–5.

In the second half of the 1958 season I drove in sixty runs and hit twenty-three home runs. I wound up hitting .269, so my average didn't come up too high. But I was very satisfied, very pleased with that second half. I had met the challenge, and overcome it.

9 I Can't Stay Mad at Frank Robinson

It took me a long while to understand Fred Hutchinson, who became manager of the Reds in 1959.

In the summer of 1958, Birdie Tebbetts resigned from the Reds. This was a shock to me. I had always felt indebted to Birdie because of what he had done for me when I was young. He had always treated me like his son. He had made it easy for me to adjust to major-league ball. I was real upset when he left. I didn't know which way to turn. Here comes another manager, I said to myself, what do I do now? I was lost.

That first other manager was Jimmy Dykes, who served out Tebbetts' term in 1958. Dykes was the same breed as Tebbetts, only looser. He was the happy-go-lucky type . . . go up there and take three swings. If you don't get them this time, go up and get them again and don't worry about it, you know. Just go out there and play.

The Reds hired Mayo Smith for the 1959 season. Only he didn't last long. We were in seventh place on July 8 with a 35–45 record and that was too much for management. Smith was fired and Fred Hutchinson came in.

My first impression of Hutch wasn't a good one. His reputation, of course, had preceded him. He had managed for Detroit and St. Louis and Seattle in the Pacific Coast League and they said about him that he wasn't a guy who threw chairs after a defeat, he threw *whole* rooms. Joe Garagiola once said of Hutch, "He's a nice guy, only his face hasn't found it out yet."

Well, every manager more or less has a quick fuse. Some people thought Birdie was soft with his players, but he wasn't, not when he had to be. I mean he sat down and if you abided by his rules, fine. But if you broke his rules, he was tough on you. Once in 1957 when I was in a slump, Birdie took me out in a late inning for a pinch-hitter. I came back to the bench and slammed my bat down. Tebbetts looked hard at me.

"Are you mad because I took you out?" he asked.

I was ready to tell him off but I checked myself fast. I swallowed and said, "I was mad because I wanted to hit."

He said sweetly, "Oh, I just wasn't sure you knew who was running this ball club."

Tebbetts could be as tough as he wanted to be, but he wasn't the type who would explode over a loss. He was wounded as bad as anyone else, but he kept it in him. He used to call his players up and say flattering things about them and pat them on the back and congratulate them.

Hutch wasn't that type at all. You could have a great day and you knew that if he was happy he might come up and say, "nice going," but it wasn't what you would call a warm, spontaneous thing. But that's the way he was.

And, at first, I didn't understand him, and maybe he didn't understand me. He was a real firm type of manager. He always had the respect of the team but it was hard for the players to really get close to him. Even his last days with the ball club, when he was dying, he would never loosen up. That was his make-up, that was the way he was, with all the ballplayers. And when he died I guess I felt as badly as anyone else on the team. We had our misunderstandings, but I had come to respect him greatly as a manager.

Actually, my first big problem in 1959 had nothing to do with the changing of the guard at Cincinnati. It had to do with the attempt to change me from an outfielder to a first baseman.

I resisted it.

The problem was that we had no first baseman. After ten

honorable years of service with the Reds, Ted Kluszewski was shipped to Pittsburgh. That left George Crowe, Walt Dropo, and Dee Fondy, all guys who were pretty much past their prime.

So they asked me to play first, just temporarily, they said. I was unhappy, but I played. I played 125 games at first base in 1959 and had the best year of my career to date.

And don't think they didn't throw that up to me when they told me in 1960 that they wanted me to play first again. "See," they said, "first base didn't affect you, it didn't hurt your hitting."

But it did affect me. When you are in a new position, people are more conscious of your mistakes. You make a bad play and the crowd hollers, "So-and-so would have made it." The crowd gets on you and it eats at you a little bit.

I made seventeen errors that year and the only first baseman in the National League who made more was Dick Stuart, who had a reputation to live up to (for the best of reasons, Dick became known variously as Dr. Strangeglove and The Great Stonefingers). I think I only made one error on a ground ball hit directly at me, a squibbler that went through my legs. But on the first-to-second-to-first double play, I was beautiful. I would take the ball and make the pivot to throw and the ball would end up behind me and all over—everywhere but second base. What I was doing was taking the glove and ball to my hand instead of my hand to the ball and glove. But in the outfield I had never had to handle that quick movement and pivot.

That was the whole thing of it. I just wasn't the kind of player that could make the transition from outfield to infield easily. In the first place I was apprehensive because of my arm. A different kind of throw is required from an infielder, and I was concerned that I might hurt my arm again. Also, I didn't have the quick reflexes and movements of the hand that an infielder needs. All ballplayers don't have the reflexes to play the infield. You have more time to think in the outfield, but in the infield you have to be a little quicker, a little more unconcerned. And my speed was different. I could move good but the initial movement wasn't quick like I felt an infielder's should be.

I was a little selfish about it, too, I admit. In 1959 I just had the idea that I wasn't yet experienced in the game of baseball. I still had to concentrate on my game. I was still learning about pitchers, about hitting, about running the bases, about playing the outfield. My argument to the Reds was that I had worked hard to become a big-league outfielder and, after three years in the majors, I felt I was near the goal. Now I was going to be shifted to a position that I didn't care too much about, that I thought would hurt my progress as a major-leaguer. So I wanted no part of the infield, except when I was up there hitting. Looking back, I would have to say it was not the most responsible attitude to take, but once I accepted the fact that I was going to play first base, I went out there to do my best. I would never go out and carry my feuds and personal feelings onto the field.

And I think my record in 1959 bears this out. I had quite a few big days. One game against the Dodgers I drove in five runs while hitting for the cycle—single, double, triple, home run. It was the first and only time I've done that. Another game against the Cardinals I hit three consecutive home runs, again the first and only time. Against the Braves' Bob Buhl in August I hit my first major-league grand-slam homer. And in a series against the Cubs I went four-for-four the first game, three-for-four the second (on four swings), and on my first at-bat in the third game, I got hit on the wrist by a pitched ball. I won't say it was deliberate but Sam Jones, who played for the Cubs at the time, told me later, "Our manager told the pitchers, 'Knock Robinson down as soon as he picks up his bat from the bat rack.'"

The Cubs weren't the only ones doing that in '59. We had a thing going with the Dodgers all year long. There was one time I got in a hassle with Clem Labine, the Dodgers' relief pitcher. He didn't like the way I slid into second trying to break up a double play and shouted something, and I shouted back. There was a lot of bench-jockeying going on, a lot of bad feeling between the two ball clubs. We hated the Dodgers and we felt Labine and some of the Dodger pitchers were throwing at us. I forgot what Labine said but we started going back and forth. He challenged me. He said to meet him after the ball game. I said fine, I'd see him after the game. But we never did meet.

Someone asked me at the time, "Why don't you bunt down the first-base line, run over pitchers who throw at you?" I said, "Well, if I bunt I'm taking something away from my team." That's the way I felt then, that's the way I feel today. I'm capable of hitting the ball out of the ball park. Why should I bunt for personal vengeance or personal revenge? And I think by doing that, the pitcher's winning the fight. That's what he wants you to do. He wants to make you mad up there and get you away from your game. But I always went ahead and took my regular swings.

And the ball fell in for me good in '59. I batted .311, with 125 runs-batted-in and thirty-six home runs. For good measure, I stole eighteen bases.

Despite playing first base, I did find 1959 more relaxing. I wasn't as tense as I had been in my first three years in the majors. I think one reason was that I finally had someone to talk to, someone who spoke my language, who liked to do the things I liked to do—taking in movies, watching TV, just sleeping.

Vada Pinson came up to the Reds in 1958 and stayed the first month of the season. He wasn't quite ready that year but he was in 1959 when, as a rookie, he led the Reds with a .316 batting average.

Vada came from Oakland, too, and went to school at McClymonds, though he was three years behind me. I met him through my boyhood pal, George Johnson. Johnson's folks and Pinson's folks were good friends and every so often Vada and I would bump into each other.

He was a pitcher in those days and I think I batted against him once or twice. But I remember coming back to Oakland after my rookie year and meeting Vada at a high school football game. This was just after he had signed as an outfielder with the Reds.

"I hear you signed as a slugger now," I said.

He said, "I'm gonna give it a try."

In 1958 he was one of the youngest ones in the Reds' camp and I knew how he felt. His first night in Tampa he checked into a Negro hotel. He was up in his room alone and a bunch of us were over at the hotel talking it up outside. Suddenly, this kid pops his head out of the window and hollers, "Hey, Frank, this is me, Vada."

I said, "What are you doing up there? Come on down here."

He came down and I said, "You can't be staying here. You're gonna stay with us." So we moved him into the boarding house where all the Negro players stayed in Tampa, and that's when we began to get close.

I remember the day Vada was told he was going back to the minors. We were in Pittsburgh and George Crowe and myself decided to see him off. Vada was pretty down. He said, "I'll see you guys. I don't think I'll be back."

I said, "You'll be back, you'll be back."

When we went up to Seattle to play that exhibition game during the All-Star break in '58—the game that meant so much to me—Vada dropped in on us beforehand. He came in our clubhouse all full of vinegar and said, "Hey, Frank, guess what?" He turned around. He was wearing no. 20, my number. I started laughing.

"What are you laughing at?" he said.

I said, "The first time I got up with that number, I got hit in the head."

That sonofagun caught me off second base in the game and

I was real glad when he joined our side in '59, and that's when we became very close friends and did a lot of things together. But he was always kind of secretive about his personal life.

I mean in the winter of 1960 I was washing my car one day in Oakland and he came by and said, "Hey, roomie, are you gonna be out here awhile?" I said I thought so. He said, "Why don't we drive down to spring training together?" I said sure. Well, I had to go back to Cincinnati and the next thing I heard, Vada had gotten married.

I couldn't believe it because he had never said a thing to me about getting married, so when he reported to camp, the first thing I did was go up to his room.

It must have been about midnight when I rapped on the door and woke him. He came to the door sleepy-eyed and said, "Good gracious, what's going on?"

I said, "Let me see your finger. Let me see it."

I looked at it and, sure enough, he was wearing a wedding band. I looked at him in disbelief. "You did do it," I said, shaking my head. "You really did do it."

He grinned. "Well, you left me, you took off without me."

The addition of Vada Pinson to our roster was one indication, I thought, that 1960 might be our year. Though we only tied for fifth place in 1959, I think we all felt we had a real good chance for the pennant in 1960. We had gotten a big year in '59 from Pinson in his rookie season, and from Johnny Temple and Gus Bell. And we had lost our shortstop, Roy McMillan, with a broken collarbone for most of '59. We thought with McMillan coming back healthy, and with some more pitching help, we might have a big year.

In the winter the Reds did make a trade for a pitcher, sending Johnny Temple to Cleveland for Cal McLish. But the trade didn't help at all, and 1960 turned out to be a bad year all-around.

It started for me in spring training. I was having the usual trouble with my arm. It always takes me a while to get the arm in shape and so I have to go easy at first. But the new manager sees those other guys out there throwing to the cut-off man in infield practice, and he figures you ought to be doing it, too. And I think Fred Hutchinson, who was new to the club as far as spring training went, resented my way of getting into shape, though he never said anything to me.

We'd been in camp for about two or three weeks and the arm was still bothering me, but it did seem to be better. I was on the sideline getting ready to go out for fielding practice. Then I felt a catch in my shoulder, up in the socket area, and I couldn't seem to get the arm loose.

I took outfield practice and I threw the ball in and the arm went on me. It didn't pop or anything, but it was very sore. So I went in and told the trainer that I'd play but couldn't throw. And I was taken out of the lineup.

The next day Fred Hutchinson blasted me in a column in a Cincinnati paper.

This is one thing Birdie Tebbetts never did. He never ripped a player in print, and I was really upset. The story quoted Hutch as saying that I had been around long enough to know I had to get my arm in shape, that I'd had this injury long enough and I should know how to take care of it and nobody told me I had to throw from the outfield. He went on to say that if I wasn't ready by Opening Day, I'd be fined for each day that I didn't play.

Well, I couldn't play in those exhibition games, and the Reds' front office didn't like that. They always wanted you to play in the first exhibition game, the second exhibition game —all the exhibition games.

To further complicate matters, I was still feuding with the management about playing first. I finally decided that if they wanted me to play first base, if they wanted me to play out of position, I should be paid extra for it.

On the morning of Opening Day, just a few hours before game time, I was in Gabe Paul's office for a last-ditch meeting to try to resolve the situation. For the thousandth time,

I was explaining to Gabe Paul why I didn't want to play first base.

Paul listened for a while, then he decided to listen no longer. He said, "You'll play first base or be suspended without pay."

I said, "Consider me suspended."

I started to walk out of the office, and he stopped me.

Finally, we worked out an arrangement over and above my contract, where I would be paid so much for each game that I played at first base.

I played seventy-eight games at first, until a bright young rookie, Gordy Coleman, was ready to take over.

It was not the best year of my life.

I started off very slow. I had a succession of minor injuries —pulled leg muscle, bad heel, ankle, thumb—and in the first half of the season I hit only .259. Once, in that period, I was benched. The explanation came from Hutch to a Cincinnati writer: I couldn't hit right-handed pitchers. So for about a two-week period I played maybe three games, all against left-handers.

Hutch made that statement to the press but he never did come over and tell me anything, or try to explain his thinking. So I said to myself, if this is how he wants to play, if he won't come to me, I won't go to him. And when the writers came to me for my version I said, "If I couldn't hit right-handed pitching I wouldn't be here today, because I hit right-handed pitching better than left-handed pitching." Then I added, "But from where I'm sitting, I can't hit nobody."

Hutch finally allowed that I could probably hit right-handers as good as left-handers and he reinstated me. One fellow who helped me with the manager at that time, as he did in later years, was Reggie Otero, a coach for Hutch. Reggie would come and talk to me and settle me down, show me both sides of things. Reggie was very close to Hutch, was able to say things to me that Hutch—because of his nature— couldn't say to me. Otero knew what this man was doing and what he was feeling, and I got a better understanding of the man through Reggie.

That was part of the problem. There were other things, too. On May 15 we played a doubleheader with the Phillies. Our pitcher, Raul Sanchez, was wild and hit three Phillies in a row, and the last one he hit was their pitcher, Gene Conley. Well, Gene Mauch, the manager, came tearing out of the dugout, and Billy Martin, our second baseman, caught Gene at the first-base line and wrapped his arms around him and was holding him pretty good. And that's when the fighting broke out.

While Martin was holding Mauch, Conley was belting Martin. Billy hit back at the six-foot-eight pitcher and said later, "Fighting him is like fighting a two-story building."

I was in it, too. A couple of the Phillie players had me down and Robin Roberts came over and made a racial comment while I was on the ground. When I got up I went looking for him and we squared off and threw a couple of punches.

Later, Roberts apologized for what he said and I accepted his apology.

We had another little battle with the Dodgers that same month. It seemed that we were always battling with the Dodgers in those days. Roger Craig was the pitcher this time and Vada was trapped off third. Jim Gilliam was running him home and he ran him too close to home plate before he threw Craig the ball. Craig was the last man between Vada scoring or being out and Vada couldn't slide—he would have cut Craig if he had slid—so he just hit Craig straight on, just ran over him, and he broke Craig's collarbone.

It was an unfortunate thing but pitchers are always susceptible to injuries when they have to come in and cover home and try to make a tag on a batter. I remember one year I came into the plate and Bob Anderson, then a pitcher with the Cubs, jumped up and came down on my arm and cut me.

If I had slid in and cut him they might have said I did it deliberately.

Well, the Dodgers were pretty upset about that even though it was clearly an accident. The next night Stan Williams was pitching, and he liked to throw at hitters.

In the seventh inning Williams threw at Vada a couple of times. Vada didn't say anything, but I did. From the on-deck circle I started hollering at Williams. "If you can't get a guy out with the natural stuff," I said, "you don't belong in the big leagues."

And he hollered back something. I couldn't make out what he said but he invited me out and both of us started at each other, and then they broke it up.

And, on the next pitch, he hit Vada on the arm.

It wasn't over. Vada stole second and went to third on a fly and he came in and scored when another Williams duster went over the batter's head into the backstop. And that's how we won that game.

After that, we were always in a war with the Dodgers. Drysdale. Craig. Williams. Labine. The duster was always flying at us. Leo Durocher, the third-base coach, was supplying his own ammunition, too. He especially liked to get on me. He said I wouldn't have hit .200 in the days when he played. He said I wouldn't even have made the clubs he played for. I gave it to him right back. I told him he was lucky he ever got into baseball—a .250 hitter at best. And it went back and forth like that all year, and into 1961, too.

Craig, in fact, hit me on the head in one game in 1960, but it just stunned me at the time and I stayed in the lineup. Other hurts had more damaging effects. One game I was sliding into home plate and I hit a shinguard and turned my ankle. A few days later, when I was just about over that one, I hurt the other ankle.

I have always been told, even in my high school days, that when you start to slide into a base, you don't hold up. It's better to go on sliding and get up and go rather than to start the slide and change your mind. But in this game I started to slide and the shortstop covering the bag dropped the ball and it rolled away from him and so I tried to hold up my slide, tag the bag and go on to third for the extra base. And I just turned the ankle. I was lucky I didn't break it, though I thought I did at the time.

So now I was playing on two bad ankles and then I got into my big August 15 fight with Ed Mathews and came out of that one battered and swollen.

One thing I would like to correct about that fight. A lot of people said later that the fight worked wonders for Frank Robinson, that it shook him out of his slump, that it made him mad, inspired him to play better ball. Well, how long can you stay mad? You can't stay mad over a 162-game schedule.

I once told a writer, "I do my damndest when I get mad at Frank Robinson." And so I do. If I've made a mistake out there, if I'm picked off base or lose a ball in the outfield or don't hit a ball I know I should hit, I get mad at myself and I'm a little more determined—as long as I can control my anger and not lose my concentration. But I can't stay mad at Frank Robinson, and I certainly can't stay mad at him over 162 games. I think I have been able to play some good baseball when I'm not mad.

Take the Mathews incident. Here's what I was doing just *before* that fight.

On August 8 I pinch-hit against the Giants (I was out at the time with a bad ankle). I singled and that led to the tying run.

On August 10 I hit a pinch-double in the eighth inning, driving in a run, later scoring the winning run in a 5–3 victory.

On August 12, I singled in the eighth, stole second, and scored the winning run against the Dodgers.

On August 14, the day before the fight, we played the Dodgers a doubleheader. We won the first game, 2–0, and I doubled home one run and scored the other. We lost the second game 9–5 but I hit two home runs and a double and drove in three runs.

So that Mathews fight really didn't trigger any great spurt on my part. The fact is I hit .341 the second half of the season. That got me up to .297, with thirty-one home runs and eighty-three runs-batted-in. These were all below my own standards but still good enough to lead the ball club in each department.

And yet when I met Mr. Bill DeWitt, the new general manager of the Reds, to talk over my 1961 contract, he was interpreting the figures a lot different. In fact, he was interpreting Frank Robinson a lot different.

From the beginning, Bill DeWitt and I never really hit it off. He came to Cincinnati as general manager after the 1960 season with a reputation, a reputation as a man who poked his nose into what was happening down on the field.

We had all heard from other players that he would come into the clubhouse right after a ball game and chew the players out for something they didn't do or something they should have done on the field. If that was true it was going to be some switch from what we were used to. Gabe Paul never came into the clubhouse and he never chewed out a player. He left that up to his manager.

But I have always tried not to judge a person on another person's information. I've always tried to wait and see for myself. And that's what I planned to do in Mr. DeWitt's case.

I was living in Cincinnati then and I was always in and out of the Reds' office. It was downtown and naturally I became very friendly with the office personnel, and I would pop in and out quite often in the off-season.

When Mr. DeWitt took over the club I just thought the right thing for him to do would be to at least call up the ballplayers, especially the ones who lived in town, and introduce himself, say hello, maybe talk a little with them. But nothing.

I met him by accident one day when I was in the office talking to the switchboard operator. He happened to come out of his office and saw me and introduced himself, the official greeting.

"I'm Bill DeWitt," he said, "nice seeing you." And we shook hands and that was it.

A few weeks later I asked to see him. I told him I'd like to sit down and talk contract with him since I was planning to go to Oakland to visit my family. He said, "I don't have the time now. I'm going to the baseball meetings and I'll be home in two weeks. See me when I get back." That was my first meeting with Mr. DeWitt and it left a little resentment, a bitter taste in my mouth.

When he came back I didn't call him and he didn't call me and when we finally did sit down to talk contract the first thing he offered me was a cut.

I didn't have the best of seasons in 1960, I admit that. But, after all, I had led the club in the three big categories— batting average, home runs, and RBI. I was making thirty thousand dollars at the time and he wanted me to take a twenty-five-hundred-dollar cut. I couldn't see it.

He just put out the cold figures. He said, "You hit .311 in 1959, you drove in 125 runs, and hit thirty-seven home runs. In 1960 you hit .297, you drove in eighty-three runs, you hit thirty-one home runs. You got to take a cut."

I told him no. I said, "Mr. DeWitt, the year wasn't that bad. It was comparable to the type of year the ball club had in 1960." I went on to show how in 1959 a lot of the players had had good years. Johnny Temple led the club in batting when he hit .316. Vada Pinson had an outstanding year. Then, in 1960, everyone was down off the figures of 1959. So was I. But I still led the club in those three main departments. And I just felt that considering the dropoff of the whole ball club, my year had been comparable to 1959. The figures weren't the same naturally, but I didn't think they were justified in cutting me.

I didn't bring it up but if he had checked the records he would have seen that the injuries didn't help my year, piling on each other as they did.

But he kept arguing away. He kept throwing figures back and forth. He compared my high salary with other players, what he said he knew other ballplayers were making. He said I was making more at this stage of my career than certain other players had at the same comparable stage. He mentioned fellows like Hank Aaron, Mickey Mantle, and Ernie Banks. I just came back and said, "Well, they probably didn't have the good years that I've had."

He said flatly, "We can't pay this." Then he talked about how we didn't draw but so many people in 1960. "We just don't have the money to pay you," he said, "and we feel that you had a bad year, an off year, and you have to take a cut."

This went on for about two hours and then he said something that I've never forgotten and that ruined our relationship forever.

He said, "I hear you don't hustle all the time."

I blew up. I said, "Have you ever seen me play?"

He said, "No, not really, not over a full season."

"Well, until you do, don't tell me that I don't always put out on the field. I do. I always put out 100 percent on the field. It may not look like it to someone sitting in the stands. It may not look like I'm doing 100 percent, but that's the way I play."

That *is* the way I play. I don't go running on and off the field at breakneck speed just because it looks good to the fans. A lot of fellows want to do that, it's okay with me. But I call it false hustle. And the way I run may not look like I'm running hard because I have that long, loping motion, and I kind of run all hunched up. But I run hard when I have to and I play hard all the time. I go into walls for fly balls because I think every ball hit within the park can be caught. And I always slide in hard to break up double plays as if every ballplayer is my enemy. And every opponent *is* my enemy. And that's the way I play—with reckless abandon.

I told all this to Mr. DeWitt at our first meeting and then he brought up the thing that has haunted me all my career— that I have to be mad to play good baseball. "The figures," DeWitt said, "showed that you played better after the Mathews incident."

"Look, Mr. DeWitt," I said. "I don't have to be mad to play good baseball. I think I proved that in my good years when I had no run-ins, or fights, with anyone."

Then he insinuated—he didn't actually say it—that he was going to keep me mad during the season. He was going to keep poking me, keep me at the boiling point, he implied, to get the best performance out of me.

When I left his office, I *was* mad. I was burned up. I finally signed the contract, for the same figure as 1960, and I said, "Just wait until next year. I'll go out and have a good year and then come back and I'll be in the driver's seat."

I left Mr. Bill DeWitt feeling that I had struck bottom in my career, and that there was only one way to go—up. I was wrong.

10 The Turning Point in My Life

I bought a gun in spring training in Florida in 1960.

It was a small gun, an Italian beretta .25—it fit right in the palm of my hand—and when I went shooting at the police firing range in Cincinnati, the cops used to make fun of it. "Did you buy that from a circus midget?" they joshed. I took one look at *their* guns and just kept quiet.

I'll tell you why I bought that gun. It was because I was twenty-four years old and not yet a man.

I was a major-league ballplayer, I was making good money, more money than I had ever seen in my life. All I had to do, I thought, was spend it. Why not? I wasn't married, I didn't have any particular responsibilities, though I always sent some money home to my mother. I just felt the money I was making was to spend. Why save it? Why put it in the bank? There would be time for that later. So I always kept a lot of money in my pocket and I spent it like water. And if I had to do it all over again I'd probably do it the same way—though, probably not for such a long period. In those first few years in the big leagues it was really something, having money to spend; it was something, after having nothing all my life.

Mostly, I spent money on cars. Oh, I spent it on my friends, too, on girls I dated, on good times. And I spent a little on clothes. I never bought fancy stuff, a lot of sweaters and sports clothes, maybe $150 at a clip, but that's all. Cars were my real weakness. I changed cars like people change shirts. As quickly as one would get old—two, three, six months—I'd

buy a new one. I'd see one that I liked, and I'd go buy another one. In 1957 alone, I think I owned five cars. I traded
in one model after driving it a thousand miles.

I was so immature in those days, typical of the kid who
never had anything and then, all of a sudden, comes into a
fortune. It was too much for me to cope with. I couldn't
handle it. I still had to grow up.

The gun, then, was for protection. At least, that's what I
thought. I don't think I ever could have used it, although
it was always loaded. It was a kid thing, really. I just felt,
I've got a gun, fine. Nobody's going to bother me. But I never
used it, except on the police shooting range.

A funny thing about that. All the time I was shooting with
the police, nobody questioned whether I had a permit for the
gun. Well, I didn't because I didn't even know one was
required. But in the state of Ohio you can't even get a permit
to carry a gun unless you have a very special reason. Nobody
told me this and I carried the gun around everywhere I
went, completely unaware of the possible consequences.

I always had large sums of cash on me—from $250 to
$2500 sometimes—and having that gun handy made me feel
better. Everybody knew that I carried a lot of money and in
those days I didn't always hang around the nicest places in
Cincinnati. In addition, I lived in an apartment house and
I had to drive around to the rear to park the car. When I shut
off the headlights, it was pretty dark. Behind the apartment
house there was a slope, an open space, and anyone could
be down there waiting for me. I could have been ambushed
walking in the dark from my car to the apartment. The
thought of that shook me a little and having the gun made
me feel more comfortable.

On the night of February 9, 1961, I played in a local
pickup basketball game. Afterwards, I drove home with two
friends. On the way we decided to stop in this little drive-in
to get a bite to eat.

It was about eleven-thirty at night and we went inside

and sat at a horseshoe-shaped counter. There were three white fellows sitting across from us but I didn't think anything about it. I ordered a hamburger and the next thing I knew one of my friends was arguing with the men across the counter.

To this day I don't know how the argument started or what it was really about. I just hadn't been paying attention. When you hear it the second time from your friends, it gets dressed up a little, so I really can't say what it was all about. But it did get nasty, and there were racial things thrown in, and they were going at it real good. So to make it equal, my friend and I stood up and said, "Well, if you guys want trouble, come on."

There was a police car in the restaurant's parking lot—two policemen waiting to be served—and someone inside called over the intercom for help.

The police rushed in and broke it up. They came up to us and the first thing one of them said was, "All right, *boys*." Now I always resent someone calling me "boy" because down South it's a polite name for "nigger." Even if they know your name down there, they call you "boy."

I spoke out. I said, "We're not boys, we're men, and that's the way you should address us if you're going to say anything to us."

I tried to speak calmly, but one of my friends got all heated up and got real loud with the police about the "boy" thing. They told him to settle down and he didn't. So they took him to the station and booked him for disturbing the peace.

We went down with him and bailed him out. I think it cost me a hundred dollars to get him out. But, naturally, I had the cash on me. Then we went back to the drive-in, and it started all over again.

The cast was the same, except the three guys we had the original argument with were gone. But we had come back to pick up our hamburgers, and the two policemen were back to get their order. When I saw their car I said to my friend, the one who had been arrested, "You go inside and get the hamburgers. We'll wait out here. And *don't* get in any more trouble."

We saw our friend talking to the cops and I said, "Oh, no, he's at it again." So we got out of the car and dashed into the restaurant. But he wasn't in any trouble. He was laughing and joking with them, and I felt better about it.

When the policemen finished their coffee, they left and we decided to sit down and have the hamburgers right there. We were eating when all of a sudden I looked into the kitchen —it's an open area and you can see right in. The chef was looking right at me. And as I watched, he took his right hand, placed it to the far side of his neck and slowly drew his hand, index finger outstretched, across his throat. The gesture was plain to me: He was going to slit my throat.

Now I had had it. Everything that had happened to me that evening seemed to well up in me, seemed to stick in my craw. In the best of times, I am not the most even-tempered soul alive, though I have always tried to retain my composure, my self-control. In those days I did have a quicker fuse than I do today. I would let things bug me till I just exploded. And when I did, I knew it was wrong. But then it's gone, then it's done, and I tried not to let it happen again.

This was one of those times. That chef's gesture just got to me. I stood up and said, "Well, come on."

He started toward me, with a butcher's knife in his right hand.

There was a partition separating the kitchen from the main dining area. It shielded him so most diners couldn't see him. But I was standing up, on the side where you could look right in to that partition, and I saw him all right. He was coming at me with that butcher's knife poised in his right hand.

I was wearing a three-quarter-length jacket, and that moment I took my gun out of my right jacket pocket. I didn't finger it, I didn't aim it at him—I merely put it in the palm of my left hand, so he could see it.

I shouted, "If you think you're a big man, come on."

He stopped short and yelled, "Hey, that guy's got a gun!"

The same two policemen were right outside the door. They hustled back in.

If I was thinking right, I would have hollered to the police myself instead of taking out my gun. I would have told them that the chef was threatening me with a cleaver. But I wasn't thinking. As they came in, I stuffed the gun back in my pocket.

One of the cops came up to me, smiling, and said—I think in a joking way—"Frank, you don't have a gun on you, do you?"

I said, "No." Another mistake. I don't know why I said no because I knew they would search me anyway. But I still said no. And they did search me and found the gun and took me to the precinct station.

They didn't book me right away because they said they had a lot of work to do. And while I waited a Cincinnati sportswriter, Earl Lawson, came over. He had evidently been tipped off by one of the cops.

Earl was very nice. He called Bill DeWitt and woke him up and tried to get Mr. DeWitt or someone to come help me. But Mr. DeWitt told Lawson he wasn't going to worry about it now, or lose any sleep over it, that he would take care of it in the morning. Then I guess he turned over and went back to sleep.

This really upset me. I didn't expect Mr. DeWitt to come down personally to get me out. But I thought at least he would get in touch with someone, the club's lawyer or somebody, and send him down to the station to bail me out. If Gabe Paul had still been general manager he would have gotten out of his bed and come over personally. And I don't think I would have been in a cell for more than two minutes.

I know this from personal experience. The only other time

in my life I ever got in trouble with the police, Gabe Paul swiftly came to my rescue.

This was in Tampa in the spring of 1958. In the evening, after practice, the Negro ballplayers, especially the single ones, would go over to the Central Avenue district. There are pool halls there and little clubs, which was about the only entertainment available to us in those days. We couldn't go out to the jai alai fronton. At the dog track we had to go downstairs and sit so far away that the dogs looked like rabbits and the rabbits like fleas. No movies, no bowling, nothing. It was watch our step every time we went on the street. So we just hung out in this one district.

One night, about 11 P.M., I was on a street corner in the area with George Crowe and Jesse Gonder. We were just standing there talking, and out of an impulse I started shaking the street-corner sign. It was a spontaneous gesture; everyone does things like that at different times in their lives and no harm is meant. But two policemen came by, saw me, and cried, "Get your hands off."

These were Negro cops and I should explain that some of the people in this Negro district resented the ballplayers. When we came to town they felt we disrupted their whole way of living. Some of the ballplayers would take girl friends for six weeks, and things like that. These cops immediately knew we were ballplayers, and that didn't help.

Well, I got mad right away. Whenever I feel that I'm right about something, I don't care what it is, I'll go all out for it, I'm going to stand up for it.

I said, "Are you kidding? I'm not doing any harm or anything."

They said, "I told you to get your hands off it."

I stopped shaking the sign now but I still had my hands on it. I said, "Look, I'm not hurting a thing. Why should I move?"

Then they grabbed me. They thrust my hands behind my

back, they hustled me up against a wall, and started to search me. I said, "What are you looking for?"

They said, "Oh, shut up and don't get smart."

I didn't say anything and one of the cops jerked me around and said, "We'll show you, we'll teach you a lesson."

Jesse spoke up then. He said, "Do you know who this is?"

They said, "We don't care who it is."

I told Jesse, "Just forget about it." I didn't put up any resistance and they took me downtown.

I wasn't permitted to use the phone but George and Jesse called the hotel and in a matter of minutes manager Birdie Tebbetts and Gabe Paul were at the station. They got me out of there right away and no charge was ever set against me.

That was the way Gabe Paul worked. He was quite a different person from Bill DeWitt. And when Mr. DeWitt went back to sleep, grouching because we had disturbed his peace, the police took me downtown to the stationhouse and booked me on the charge of carrying a concealed weapon.

They put me in a detention cell. It was a real odd feeling hearing the door close behind me and the key turning. The cell was hot and I took off my jacket and bunched it on a bench, which was the only piece of furniture in the room. And I lay down and tried to sleep.

But sleep didn't come. I had a lot of things to think about. At first I wondered how I was going to get out, and when. When the ball club was going to make my bail. Was somebody going to come down and get me out?

Then I thought about how this might affect my baseball career. I wondered what the president of the National League might do to me. He could put me out of baseball if he wanted, and I was worried about that.

But the most disturbing thought of all, the one that haunted me all night long, was, what the kids would think of me.

So many kids idolize big-league ballplayers. So many of

them mold their whole lives around their heroes. What were they going to think? How were they going to react?

And then it began to dawn on me, that I had a responsibility to the game of baseball. Baseball had been good to me and I had taken a lot out of it, but what had I given back? I felt a deep responsibility to baseball, especially to the young kids who look up to the players. I felt that I had let them down.

For the first time I began to realize that I wasn't a kid any more and that I better stop acting like one. I knew that I had been wrong, dead wrong, all the way. But looking back, it may have been the best thing that ever happened to me. It matured me, it made me a better man. No, not a better man—a man. Let me put it that way because I don't think I was a real man before.

The next morning I was released on a bond of $1000. Three weeks later I faced a grand jury. I pleaded guilty to carrying a concealed weapon and was fined $250.

By this time I was in training camp, preparing for the 1961 season. I still remember the only words that my manager, Fred Hutchinson, ever spoke to me of the incident. The first day he saw me in Tampa he strode right up to me. He looked me cold in the eye and said:

"That was a stupid thing to do."

"It was," I said, "but sometimes a man learns from his stupidities."

I faced a new baseball season gripped by two feelings—fear and determination. The fear was what the gun incident would mean to the fans. I don't mean I was worried about the fans getting on me. I expected them to ride me and heckle me—and they did. But I was concerned about the kids, about the effect it would have on them.

And my determination came out of that fear. I vowed to have the best year of my life, to show those kids something, to show them—and everyone—that I was more mature as a ballplayer, and as a man.

11   Happiness Is a Pennant

When I reported to Tampa in late February of 1961, the first thing I saw in my locker was a water pistol. Ed Bailey had put it there, and that water pistol to me was the keynote of the whole 1961 season.

I picked up the pistol gingerly and carried it over to Bailey, who was standing by his locker playing dumb. "Thanks, Eddie," I said gravely, "but I can't use it. I'm on parole."

That was the beginning, only the beginning. When we went over to Bradenton to play the Braves an exhibition game, I was shagging flies in left field. Nearby, on the porch of the Braves' clubhouse, Felix Mantilla and Henry Aaron were singing a duet at the top of their voices:

Lay that pistol down, babe, lay that pistol down.

Lew Burdette, who was something of a clown when he was not pitching, crept up on me and started frisking me. Very professional, too. "It's all right, Eddie," Burdette hollered to Ed Mathews, "he's clean."

Mathews, remembering our little boxing match the previous season, said, "Hey, Robby, I'm not fooling around with you this year."

What could I do but grin sheepishly at these guys and keep my mouth shut. Ordinarily, I'm a pretty good needler myself, but this was a case where anything I said would be used against me. So I took the fifth. It was good-natured practical joking, anyway, and I didn't mind that. What I didn't enjoy particularly was the fans getting on me, especially the kids. But I got used to hearing them holler, "Where's your gun?"

or, "Hey, Colt .45!" or, "Who do you think you are—Wyatt Earp?"

When I'd argue with an umpire over a called strike or a close play at a base, I'd trot out to the outfield later and hear, "Why didn't you pull your gun on him?" But I was expecting that kind of stuff, I knew I was going to get it, and I made up my mind that I wasn't going to let it bother me.

Rather than bother me, all those remarks, all that jockeying, served a purpose. It was like waving a red flag in front of me constantly. It was a reminder, a goad. With what had happened to me over the winter, I knew in 1961 I had to have a good year. I couldn't afford to have a bad year. It might have endangered my entire baseball career.

It was the year I just had to grow up. Now I was going on twenty-six, a five-year veteran of the Cincinnati ball club, and almost the senior player in point of service (Gus Bell and Wally Post had been with the Reds longer but they were now part-time players). This was a goad, this told me I better get going, that I had a responsibility to this ball club.

I think the gun incident woke me to those responsibilities, made me reflect on where I was trying to go, on what I was going to do with my good fortune in playing in the major leagues. Some people after all never get the chance to play in the major leagues. I asked myself, am I letting it all slip through my fingers? Am I really accomplishing anything?

And I joined the club that spring and began to hear the talk about me being its leader. Mind you, I didn't move in that spring of 1961 and say, okay fellers, your leader is here. It was more someone else putting the tag on me. But if that's the way they felt (the manager, the general manager, some of the players, the press), then I felt I owed it to my teammates to perform as more of a leader. I mean not just my hitting and fielding and running—I always played hard that way—but my speaking up a little bit more, the way I carried myself on the field, and the things I did off the field.

Spring training of 1961 was like no other I had ever experienced. It was more than my personal conversion, my new attitude toward the game of baseball. There was something in the air and it was infecting all of us. It was a feeling that we were going somewhere this year, really going somewhere in the pennant race.

First of all, we came up with some good young fellows, like Johnny Edwards, who became our no. 1 catcher; Chico Cardenas, who was just starting to play shortstop; and Gordy Coleman, who would become a full-time first baseman, which would leave the left-fielding to me.

In trades we got Gene Freese from the White Sox to play third base for us, Don Blasingame from the Giants to help Elio Chacon at second, and Joey Jay from the Braves, to give us more pitching strength.

Around them were the veterans: Vada in center field, just coming into his strength; Eddie Kasko, who played short mostly; Bell, Post, and Jerry Lynch in the outfield; Pete Whisenant, who was a utility infielder and our no. 1 cheerleader; Bob Purkey, an experienced pitcher who had won seventeen games for us in 1960 and seemed to be at the peak of his career; and Jim O'Toole, who had been up since 1958 and seemed about ready to come into his own.

On paper, this didn't seem to be a very imposing lineup, and the press got to calling us "ragamuffins" as we kept winning ball games. The press, in fact, had pretty much figured it out before the season: we would be good for another sixth-place finish. Well, that gave us a little extra incentive. We felt that we were a good club, now we wanted to prove it. We were going to win and that's all there was to it. It was like the kid who goes home and swipes the cookies out of the cookie jar and they never miss them and he goes around the corner and laughs about it.

We broke well by winning our first five of seven games, and then we lost eight in a row. Other seasons we'd have folded and died right there. But we won our next nine in a row and I remember thinking, maybe we'll scare hell out of a few teams before we're through.

For a change I got off to a pretty good start. I had had a good exhibition season and, for the first time in years, my arm was in real good shape—thanks to a big, ex-college football coach, Otis Douglas.

Douglas had been hired by the Reds to get the ball club in condition, and he did just that, though he nearly killed us in the process. He had us doing pushups and situps and all sorts of impossible exercises that baseball players are never supposed to do. He had us out there until our tongues were hanging out and we were screaming for mercy. But then he would come around and work on my arm and that made up for all his tortures. He had real strong hands and he was able to massage my arm and dig down deep and break up the knots that always formed in the arm, and he got it in good shape.

One game in April I got Willie Mays trying for second after tagging up at first on a fly ball caught in left. We won the game by a run. Any other year we would have been tied going into extra innings because I wouldn't and couldn't have cut loose and Willie would have scored on the base hit that followed.

Another game that month, Sandy Koufax came up. He was a very poor hitter and I was cheating a little, playing in much closer than I should. And he hit a line drive between first and second. I charged the ball, took it on the first hop and threw to first base for the out. I think Sandy was a bit surprised about that. I know the next time the Dodgers came in, he made a point to come over to me and register a complaint. "Frank," he grumbled, "as hard as hits are for me, I finally get one and you take it away from me."

That's the way things were going for me at the beginning. I even stole third when a pitcher was intentionally walking a hitter. That happened early in the season. Bob Friend of the Pirates was walking Gene Freese. I watched Friend closely.

He wasn't taking a very good look at me on the first three pitches, so on the fourth I took off for third and made it.

Through mid-May I was batting close to .300 with about ten home runs. I was in a pretty good groove, and then the pitchers got in their groove against Frank Robinson.

We were playing the Braves a doubleheader on May 21. I had singled, walked, and homered. My fourth time up in the seventh inning, Claude Raymond hit me on the back of my arm and that was the hardest I've ever been hit on any part of my body, except my head. I don't think he hit me deliberately. I think he was trying to get in tight and the ball just ran in on me.

It ran in all right, in back of my bicep, and it really hurt. I must have stayed around home plate for two or three minutes. Normally, I'm able to shake off these things, but this was different. I went to first base but I almost passed out, it hurt that bad, and I had to leave the game.

I had the arm X-rayed, but nothing was broken and I was in the lineup the next day.

For a while, though, that sore spot was like a magnet, drawing balls and bats to it.

We were playing in Philadelphia on May 27. Tony Gonzalez hit the ball to left field with good power. I was playing back deep enough, I thought, but I had to move. It was just one of those plays when you're on the dead run and you catch the ball over your shoulder. And just as I caught the ball, I hit the scoreboard going to my right and I hit that sore spot on that left arm. I was thankful that scoreboard was made of tin and had a little give in it, but the arm was real painful again and swelled up so big you couldn't see the dips.

Then we went into San Francisco for a four-game series with the Giants. On May 29, I hit a three-run homer and we beat the Giants, 5-1. That was my twelfth home run of the season, and brought my RBIs to thirty.

The next day, Memorial Day, in the first game of the

doubleheader, Jim Duffalo hit me on my trouble spot. I had to leave the game. I took whirlpool treatments in our clubhouse and between games manager Fred Hutchinson said, "We'll rest it." I told him no, I was ready to go. I took a couple of pain pills and tried to stay in but the wind was blowing pretty good and my arm stiffened up and I couldn't swing a bat. I came out in the fifth.

For about two weeks the arm was so sore I couldn't bend it enough to touch my nose. And my batting average began to go the other way.

I came out of it pretty good by mid-June.

Just at this time, we went into first place in the National League. From June 15 until the All-Star break, we won twenty-one of twenty-eight games, and went out in front by five games.

One big series came against our classic rivals, the Dodgers, on June 23, 24, and 25. In the first game I hit a home run off Don Drysdale in the sixth inning which tied the score. We went on to win it.

We lost the next game 9–7, though I had a good game. I doubled in the second off Sandy Koufax. In the third I doubled again with the bases loaded. In the fourth I was intentionally walked. In the seventh I doubled once more.

The third game I went hitless but I did cut down Jim Gilliam trying to score on a Maury Wills double and we won 3–2.

In that period I was about as hot as I had ever been in my life. In a three-game series against the Cardinals, I had eight hits in twelve times up and drove in eight runs. At one point I reached base seventeen out of nineteen times.

I think my improvement as a hitter was part of that whole growing-up process. I was maturing as a hitter, learning a little bit more about the game, thinking a little bit more about my hitting. I'd go up there with a plan, with an idea of what the pitcher was trying to do with me, what he had gotten me out on before and what I was going to look for. I was thinking all the while. I asked myself things like, What's the situation on the bases? What's the best way to bring the man home? What kind of a hit do we need? I didn't swing at the first strike as often as I had in the past. I tried to get the two-and-nothing count so I could become a guess hitter; that is, look for my pitch in this situation.

I don't like to do this too often because I'm a better hitter when I hit what I see. But, naturally, if you have three balls and one strike, you're looking for the pitch you can hit best. For me, it was the fast ball. When I got ahead of the pitcher, I usually look for nothing but the fast ball and if I get it I should be able to handle it. I should be able to hit the ball hard somewhere.

But that's not all I was thinking about. I would say to myself, under these circumstances, do I want to swing at the fast ball if it's coming over the *right corner* of the plate? I've often told myself, if you don't get the fast ball exactly where you want it—not just get it, but in the area where you want it—you shouldn't swing at it. A lot of times I swung at it anyway. A lot of times, too, I'll say I'm looking for a fast ball and they throw a curve ball and I still swing at it. It's mind over matter sometimes. You see these balls and they look good and you swing anyway. But the majority of times when I'm ahead of the pitcher, I always look for the fast ball.

And that's what I mean by maturing as a hitter. It all came to me with experience. I thought I was doing this kind of thing before, but I wasn't really. And maybe that's the reason a lot of people said in those early years that I didn't put out. But if I didn't go up there with a plan, it was from inexperience. No one ever told me these things. I had to figure them out for myself after I left high school. I had to learn this all myself and it just took a while.

The month of July I batted .409, with thirteen home runs and thirty-four runs-batted-in. But it wasn't just me. The whole ball club was playing inspirational ball. Vada was having a great year, Gordy Coleman was driving in big runs. Joey Jay was our leading pitcher, and Jim O'Toole right behind him. And Jim Brosnan was our big man in the bullpen.

Jim Brosnan. He was the literary light of our ball club, the man who wrote books on the side. In 1960 he wrote a book called *The Long Season*. In it he made certain references to me that were not of the most complimentary nature. One thing he wrote was that I didn't play up to my ability, I didn't put out at all times. He said if he were general manager of the Cincinnati ball club, he would trade me for two ordinary ballplayers. Well, fine. Broz had played half a season with me when he sat down to write that book. But he must have felt that it didn't take very long to become an expert on when Frank Robinson was putting out and when Frank Robinson wasn't putting out. He was completely wrong, of course. Maybe I did have a couple of slumps during the year, maybe I didn't hit forty or fifty home runs. But everyone has slumps, even the so-called superstar; and I never considered myself a real superstar. Also in those years, as I have said, I felt that I was still learning about myself and about baseball. In fact, I still feel that I'm learning. Each year I try to do something a little different, or apply something that I've learned the year before to improve my performance.

Another thing Brosnan wrote about me: I'm a hard man to get to know, he said, I'm not the type of person you go out to have a beer with. Aside from the fact that I detest beer, I don't remember Jim ever asking me out to have a beer with him, so how did he know if I would have gone or not. Besides, in those days, the white players would go their way after a game and the Negro players would go their way.

So in one breath, Brosnan says I'm a hard man to know, and in another, he's got me all figured out and is ready to trade me for two ordinary ballplayers.

It's a funny world we live in because Brosnan later wrote

another book, *Pennant Race*, about the 1961 season, and
he had me all figured out again—only quite differently. Now
he was writing to the effect that it wasn't so much that I
was the leader, but that I *thought* I was the leader and that
charged me up. Wrong again, Jim.

As I said, I never thought I was the leader. It was always
someone else putting this tag on me. Fred Hutchinson said
in 1961 that I was the kind of leader Joe DiMaggio was. That
was very kind of Hutch but what I think he meant was that
I was leading by example. It was the way I was playing baseball, and if that rubbed off on the other players and made
them want to do a little extra, fine. But that's the way I always played baseball. I always wanted to be the one who put
out just a little bit more. I think I set a better example if I
was putting out more. Maybe some of the other players
were looking up to me or watching me and because I put
out a little extra, they would too.

The difference in 1961 was that I was more aware of my
responsibilities because of my seniority; and I was more determined than ever because of that gun incident, because
I had come so close to blowing my whole professional baseball career.

Example. In 1960 I stole thirteen bases and was caught
six times. In 1961, I stole twenty-two bases and was thrown
out only three times. But, again, how do you divide that improvement between my newly found determination, and my
growing experience? I was a better baserunner because I had
been watching the major-league pitchers over a period of
years, I knew them better, I could get a better jump on them,
and I was using better judgment on the bases.

Whether it was heightened desire or heightened experience, it was working for me all right. One game against the
Dodgers, Duke Snider was playing right field and I hit a
routine ground ball between first and second. I was running
real good from the time I hit the ball. Snider was slow getting
to the ball and I just kept going. I turned a routine single

into a double. That was new for me but Vada Pinson, for one, had always been doing that. In 1959 he led the league with forty-seven doubles. I think he must have turned fifteen or twenty singles into doubles by just doing what I did against Snider.

We were all taking chances on the bases in 1961, and winning games that way. Once Vada won a game for us by stealing home with two out in the ninth inning, breaking a 1–1 tie. He would have been out but he kicked the ball out of the hands of Milwaukee catcher Sammy White. Jerry Lynch had been the pinch-hitter at the plate at the time. Vada asked me later if he had made the right play and I told him it was a good play except for one thing. Lynch was up there to hit. He wasn't going to be put out in the field to play defense. So if Vada had been thrown out, Lynch, our best pinch-hitter, would have been wasted.

Judgment is so important in these instances. There was another game against the Dodgers (why is it that all my big moments seem to have come against the Dodgers?). Drysdale was pitching and we weren't doing much with him. In the third or fourth inning I singled and got to third base. Then, with one out, someone hit a pop fly. Jim Gilliam was at second base, on the edge of the outfield grass, and he caught the ball and I knew I wasn't going anyplace on that fly ball. There wasn't any sense in going halfway because what were his chances of dropping a little pop fly?

So when he was under it, I decided to go back and just tag up and maybe I would be able to steal this run. So I went back and tagged up and as soon as he caught the ball, I came off third base. He kept faking and faking and I kept jogging toward home a little, just inching off a little bit more. Finally, he dropped his arm and I took off, and by the time he got the ball to the catcher, it was a bad throw. I scored the run. They went on to beat us 5–1, but it was a big run at the time.

They did try to get me to exert some leadership off the field, too. Pete Whisenant would always come to me. "Get on those guys out there," he would say. "Don't let them mope. Keep them alive and kicking all the way. They'll look up to you."

And I went along with Whisenant as much as I could. The biggest moment came in July. We played the Cubs a four-game series and they swept the last three games, and none of us seemed to have played up to our ability. We seemed to have gone out there with the idea that the Cubs were going to give us the games, anyway, and that to beat them all we had to do was show up. We just weren't putting out, so we called a meeting of the players.

This was something we had begun in 1960, with the permission of the manager. In those days Hutch could get pretty mean in meetings—he hated so much to lose, especially when we lost because of bad mistakes—and sometimes the ball-players resented that. Hutch might point the finger at one individual and say, "you're not doing this and you're not doing that." It bothered certain players to be criticized like that in a group meeting. But we didn't call our own meetings just to stop Hutch from having a meeting and getting on our backs. It was just that we felt we were the type of team that could sit down among ourselves and work out our problems a little better, rather than having the manager sitting down and chewing us out.

In 1961 we had maybe four or five meetings where the manager and coaches weren't involved. I never called one myself, I always went through channels. Bob Purkey was the player representative and I would always go to Bob and say, "Don't you think it would be a good idea if we had a meeting?" He would either say, yes, it's a good idea, or yes, but let's cool it for a day or two and wait for the right time. And Purkey would always call the meetings.

So we held this meeting in the visiting clubhouse in Chicago before taking off for Milwaukee. I got a lot off my chest then. I said, let's stop making excuses for each other; we're playing lousy ball. Let's start thinking about correcting our mistakes. I admitted my mistakes and told them what I thought were theirs. I told off the pitchers who weren't thinking about what they were throwing when they got behind batters. I told off the batters who weren't thinking about what they were going to do when they got up to the plate. I told off the fielders about the mistakes they were making.

We were all making mistakes. I confessed that maybe I was swinging at too many bad pitches, that I wasn't waiting for my pitch to hit, and I wasn't moving the runner over. "You other hitters," I said, pointing to several of my teammates, "are hitting the first pitch too often, and swinging at a lot of bad balls and letting the pitcher get ahead of us with men in scoring position, men on bases."

The pitchers were making mistakes, too, and they admitted them. Say Ernie Banks was up to hit and first base was open. Our pitchers weren't working on him enough. They would get behind him and give in to him rather than walk him. Even when they were ahead of a batter with two strikes and no balls, the batter would wind up getting hits. I think that's one of the worst sins a pitcher can commit, letting a batter get a hit on a two-strike, no-ball count.

So that's exactly what the meeting was all about, to cleanse our souls, and it seemed to do some good because we went into Milwaukee and swept the series and went on to win ten of our next twelve games.

Still, we were never able to pull ahead in that pennant race. The Dodgers were staying right with us. And just before the All-Star break, we met the Dodgers in a four-game series, at the Los Angeles Coliseum.

We held a three-game lead at the time, and it stretched to five games when we swept a doubleheader from the Dodgers. But then we lost the third game, and that put us four ahead.

In the fourth game we led 7–2 in the sixth inning when Don Drysdale came in to pitch in relief.

Now Drysdale had been one of my biggest problems, especially in my early years in the National League. Each game that I played against him was like fighting a bear. He was six feet six, a big, rangy guy and especially tough when you were hitting from the right side. It was an awful sight to see him come off the mound and sidearm you. You really got tired after hitting against him three or four times in a ball game because on every pitch you had to really bear down and be aware of what was going on. And he was so tough. His ball would run in on you and then when you looked for the ball in on you, he would throw the hard slider over the outer part of the plate. Then when you were looking for that slider out there, he would come up and in on you. You had to be on your toes all the time, and he hit me on the fists quite a number of times getting the ball in on me.

He hit me in a lot of other places, too. In my baseball career, through 1966, pitchers have hit me 128 times. Don Drysdale is the undisputed leader in the get-Frank Robinson sweepstakes. And as the years went by and I would get hit regularly by Drysdale, the newspapers built the thing up between us, and blew it out of proportion. The fact is I respect Drysdale tremendously. He's a real competitor and that's the way it should be. He was out there trying to get me out, and my job was to get hits off him. Don felt that if he was consistently going to get me out, he had to come inside, in tight, and I knew there were times when he did hit me that he wasn't throwing at me.

But there were also those times when I knew he was throwing at me deliberately.

And that's what happened this game in July. The first Reds batter in the sixth was Don Blasingame, a left-handed hitter. The first pitch was behind his head.

Drysdale eventually got Blasingame out and the next hitter was Vada Pinson. And Vada had to skip rope three times before he finally hit one off the fist and blooped it over third base for a double. And you could just see Drysdale on the mound, the steam coming out of his ears. He was really hot about that type of a hit.

I was the next hitter and Drysdale's first pitch low-bridged me. It was either hit the dirt or take it on the head. I hit the dirt. The next pitch was right at my ribs and I had to go down again to get out of the way. After that one the umpire, Dusty Boggess, went out to Drysdale.

"That's enough of that," he said. "If you do it one more time, you're out of there."

Well, Boggess came back behind the plate and hardly had time to get his mask back on when the next pitch hit me on the forearm. The umpire stepped from behind the plate yelling, "You're gone!" and Drysdale was ejected from the game. He was fined fifty dollars and suspended for three days. We went on to win the game 14–3. And it was one of my best days ever; I went four-for-four, with two home runs, a double and a single and seven runs batted in. And now we had a five-game lead at the halfway mark.

That lead looked very good to us but we came back after All-Star time and, suddenly, we were not playing the type of ball we played the first half of the season and the lead began shrinking. On top of that the Dodgers got hot, winning nineteen of twenty games in one stretch. And on August 15 they were in first place, and we were second.

We went into the Coliseum for another big series with the Dodgers, who now led the league by two games. Joey Jay pitched the first game and won, 5–2 (I doubled to tie the score in the fifth). That put us one game behind.

The next day we played a twi-night doubleheader against them. A crowd of 72,140 turned out, the biggest crowd ever to watch a National League twi-nighter up to that time. In the first game Bob Purkey pitched a four-hit shutout and we won, 6–0. I went two-for-four, with a run scored and a run batted in.

In the second game Jim O'Toole pitched a two-hit shutout. I hit a home run and drove in two runs in the 8–0 victory.

We left the Coliseum in first place again and the Dodgers seemed to have had it. They went on to lose ten games in a row.

But they weren't finished. We began playing lousy ball again, and they began playing better ball and they came into Cincinnati for a four-game series right on our tail.

Sandy Koufax pitched a four-hitter in the opener. The next day the Dodgers won 10–6. That brought us to a double-header. If the Dodgers swept those two games they would go back into first place.

In the first game we were behind 5–1 going to the last of the seventh. I personally felt that if we lost that ball game, the way we were playing we wouldn't win the pennant in 1961.

But we turned it around. Gene Freese hit a three-run homer in the seventh to put us one run behind. In the eighth Chico Cardenas tripled in the tying run and Wally Post hit a pinch-double bringing in Cardenas, and we won it, 6–5.

We won the second game, 8–3, and now we felt there was no way the Dodgers could catch us.

Yet in early September there they were again, only one game behind us. This time we were playing the Cardinals at home.

At that moment, I wasn't hitting well at all. I went out early that night and took fifteen minutes of private batting practice. But it didn't seem to help, and going to the eighth inning we were two runs behind and I had done nothing.

Then we got a rally going. We got the tying run on with two out. I dried my hands with the resin bag and threw the weighted bat away and went up to hit.

Ernie Broglio was the Cardinal pitcher and he kept jamming me with low, inside fast balls and the count went to two and two. Then I fouled off about five pitches in a row. On the last one it was like somebody struck a match in my left hand. The skin was tender from all the batting practice and a blister broke on my middle finger.

I asked for time-out and the Cincinnati trainer, Doc Rhode, came out and put a Band-Aid on it.

The time-put was just what I needed to think over the situation, and plan what to do next. Broglio's plan was to keep jamming me, but this time he came in higher than he wanted to and I got around on the ball pretty good. I pulled it high against the scoreboard in left-center for a double and it was a tie game. We won on a single by Eddie Kasko and the Dodgers lost and we were two games ahead.

The next night we went extra innings with the Cardinals. Al Cicotte was working in relief and in the twelfth, Chico Cardenas led off against Cicotte with a double. The next two batters struck out. But then he walked Vada.

No sooner did I move in then Cicotte slipped two quick strikes by me. But he tried to sneak another strike by me and I got around on this good, too. I pulled it to the base of the scoreboard and Cardenas came in with the tying run. The Dodgers lost again and now we were three games ahead.

On September 26 we played the Chicago Cubs. We were down 3–2 in the seventh when I hit a two-run homer. Jerry Lynch hit a two-run homer in the eighth, and that was it. That night the Pirates beat the Dodgers, and the National League pennant was ours.

It's hard for me to explain what that pennant meant to me. It's a tremendous honor for an individual to play on a championship team, and the first one is the biggest thrill of all. I don't think you can ever recapture the feeling. I don't care how many pennants you win, the first one is always the greatest thrill.

Especially winning it with this ball club. I really had pride about this team, not only because we did win the pennant, and I had a big hand in it, but because we weren't picked to win. People just didn't think we could do it and we went out and showed them. And that's what I remember, and that's what this really meant to me.

There were so many great individual performances, I can't catalogue them all. I had my best year ever with a .323 average, thirty-seven home runs, 124 runs batted in. But look at what some of the other fellows did: Vada Pinson finished second in the batting race with a .343 average; Gordy Coleman drove in eighty-seven runs and hit twenty-six homers; Gene Freese hit twenty-six homers with eighty-seven RBIs; Joey Jay won twenty-one games; Jim O'Toole won nineteen. The author, Jim Brosnan, won ten coming out of the bullpen. It was a team effort all the way, fine all-around individual performances, and a top job of managing by Fred Hutchinson.

It would have been nice to have kept going through the World Series, but it wasn't to be. The Yankees beat us in five games.

But that Series was closer than it sounds.

I went into the World Series in something of a slump. During the month of September I batted .325 but I know I wasn't hitting the ball the way I could. I could have been a little tired, I don't know. I think when most players go into a slump toward the end of the season it's because they're tired and are doing things a little differently than they would ordinarily. I think that's what brings on a lot of slumps. You get tired and things don't come naturally. You have to push a little bit and pretty soon you're in a rut and you're not doing things the way you normally do. It may have been that way with me, I don't know. I do know I only got three hits in the Series for a .200 batting average. Something was wrong.

Not many of us, in fact, performed at our peaks in the Series, and I think inexperience may have had something to do with it. I had never been in a World Series before, neither had the majority of our players. It wasn't that we were scared, it was just that we weren't prepared. The Yankees were a real experienced ball club and we weren't. I think that was the real difference, that and Whitey Ford.

He was magnificent, the real big guy in that Series. He shut us out in the first game and he shut us out in the fourth game, and we just couldn't touch him. But I think the whole Series revolved around one play in the third game.

After Ford beat us, 2–0, in the opener, we came back and took the second game, 6–2, with Joey Jay pitching a four-hitter. In the third game Bob Purkey was pitching a strong game and we were leading 1–0 going into the seventh (I had driven in that run in the third with a double).

In that seventh, Tony Kubek opened with a single and moved to second on a passed ball. Then Roger Maris flied out and Mickey Mantle struck out and Yogi Berra hit a pop fly to short right field. Elio Chacon, our second baseman, was holding toward first base and came out after it at an angle. I came straight in on the dead run and actually I didn't see Chacon until the last second. I had a shot at catching the ball, but I would have had to dive for it and I might have caught it and I might not have. But Chacon seemed to have the best shot at it and I think he did have the ball in his glove just a second before I hit him. And when I ran into him, he dropped the ball and Kubek scored the tying run.

If Chacon had held onto that ball I'm convinced we would have gone on to win that game, and possibly the Series. As it was, they went on to beat us, 3–2.

Whitey Ford shut us out in the fourth game, 7–0, and they ran us out of the ball park in the fifth game, 13–5.

I did hit a home run in that last game. We were losing 6–0 in the third when I caught hold of a Ralph Terry curve and put it into the right-center-field corner of the bleachers. There were two men on so that made it 6–3 and brought us back into the game a little. As it turned out, we lost the game badly and the home run kind of got lost in the shuffle. But I'll always remember that home run, just knowing I had hit a home run in a World Series.

Early in November I was in California when a sportswriter called me.

His first words were, "Frank, you've won the Most Valuable Player award."

I was speechless. It really took me by surprise. I really didn't think I could win it. I had figured myself about third because Orlando Cepeda had had a tremendous year with the Giants, leading the National League in home runs and runs batted in, and Vada also had that great year. I honestly thought the two of them had the best shot at it.

Winning the MVP was a tremendous thrill. It's a tremendous thrill to be the best of anything in the major leagues, but this was something special. My team had also been the best in the league. You always want to have a good year, but you also take a lot of pride in what your team does. If you have a good year and the team doesn't do anything, that takes away something from your performance. In 1961, the greatest year of my life to date, my team was the best in the league and I was named the best player in the league. You can't do much better than that.

12   I Retire from Baseball

Very late in the 1962 season, I told Cincinnati sportswriter Earl Lawson that I was retiring from the game.

Well, that one created quite a stir. All over the country, newspapers proclaimed—"Frank Robinson Quitting Baseball."

It was not a gag. When I told Lawson of my decision, I had every intention of sticking to it.

I had, I thought, good reasons for quitting baseball. It had to do with the accumulation of injuries, with the heavy disappointment I felt when we failed to win the pennant in 1962 . . . and with my wife, Barbara.

Barbara Ann Cole was her maiden name. She was twenty years old when I met her, a Los Angeles girl who worked for the telephone company.

It was in August of 1961 after a ball game in the Los Angeles Coliseum. Vada and I were coming out of the gate and I met a friend of mine, a fellow from Oakland, who was going to drive us back to the hotel. His car was parked in the parking lot and as we were crossing the lot we saw two girls standing there. One, Barbara Ann Cole, the other her sister.

My friend knew Barbara and he introduced Vada and me to both girls. It seemed that they had taken their uncle to the ball game—he was from out-of-state—and he was supposed to meet them in a certain spot in the parking lot. But he was lost. So they went around looking for him and that's the way I bumped into Barbara.

Well, we went out then and got something to eat and we talked a long time. And it didn't take me more than five minutes to feel that I had known her all my life.

It's always been my theory that you can get to know a person in five minutes, that you don't have to know a person two or three months or two or three years to really know them. How long really do you have to know a person to *know* them? You can be a lifetime knowing a person and not really know him, and you can meet him and, in a few minutes, feel that you know him intimately.

And that's how it was with Barbara and me.

We talked for quite some time that first night and, after that, we burned up the long-distance phone lines talking just about every day. My roomie, Vada Pinson, began to wonder what was up. One day, just before the World Series, I told Vada and some of the other guys, "All right, we got to win this. I need the money."

"Why?" asked Vada.

"I'm gonna get married."

"Are you serious?"

"Remember," I said, "I don't fool around."

And I didn't, not this time. We were married on October 28, 1961.

At first, married life was quite an adjustment for me. I guess it's the same with all old-line bachelors. I was used to living alone and being able to go and do things whenever I wanted to. I was the type who would wake up late in the morning, grab the morning paper, and look to see what movie was playing downtown. I'd get something to eat and go to the movie. And at night, after a ball game, I might go out for a while, or have friends over, and just do what I wanted.

So that part took some adjusting. I think that was really the tough part of it, knowing that there was someone else I had to consider, and share my thoughts with. That's the way my life changed—but it changed for the better. It settled me down. I think it made me a better person.

Barbara has influenced my life immensely. Now, instead of carrying a lot of money around in my pocket, I have to dig deep to see if I have two quarters to rub together. After

I was married I went two years without buying a car—a world record for me—and I actually had to live on a *budget*. But that helped settle me down. I began to eat regular meals, good well-balanced meals (Barbara's a tremendous cook), and it just settled me down. It was more than that, of course. It was someone who you were very close to, someone to talk to and who understands the way you feel and knows when something is bothering you and when things aren't going well.

Another stabilizing influence in my life has been our kids. We were married eleven months when we decided to adopt a baby. By this time we felt we wanted a child; we hadn't been told that we couldn't have kids of our own, but we just felt we wanted one now. So we talked it over and decided that we would adopt one. I think what really brought it about was Barbara's sister. They had a son, then adopted a little girl. And she was a real doll.

Frank Kevin was actually nine months old when we got him. The adoption agency tries to get a kid who will fit into the family, who will look somewhat like you, and be of the same disposition as you. They brought out some pictures and let us look at the children. They said they would bring one kid out and let us look at him and then they would take him back and bring another. Well, the first boy they brought to us was Kevin. They showed him to us and said, "Well, we'll bring another one out."

We said, "Nope, we'll take him." He was the first one we saw and we loved him right away.

Then, in August of 1965, Barbara had a baby girl who we named Nichelle. That really completed the family. It gave us a boy and a girl. Barbara was so happy. When she was pregnant she said to me she wanted a girl, "someone around the house when you're gone who'll help me and talk to me." We were happy the first one was a boy so he could look after his little sister. Having those kids really made a difference. It filled out our lives.

But in the summer of 1962 we hadn't been married a year yet and there were no kids and I was a little worried about Barbara. She didn't know too much about baseball, she didn't understand the inner workings of baseball, like the traveling, my being away from home two or three weeks at a time, the spring training when I was gone for six weeks, things like that. She had never really been away from her family. We had gotten married in Los Angeles and had gone right back to Cincinnati, to a strange city for her. And she didn't know too many people. When I was on the road, she was home all by herself. It bothered her, she was a little afraid at times, and it affected me and I felt that maybe this was the thing to do, get out of baseball if it was going to upset her so. Maybe this was the best time for me to get out of the game and into something else if it was going to make her unhappy with me still in baseball.

These were all my own thoughts, mind you. Barbara had never said anything to me. She had never suggested that I get out of the game. It was just something I sensed. I didn't even talk it over with her. This was my decision and she was as surprised as anybody when she saw it in the paper.

And, as I say, it wasn't just Barbara. It wasn't any single thing. Just the thought of missing out on the pennant, the injuries starting to pile up and now a little harder to shake than they were in the earlier years. I thought of my responsibilities as a family man. What if I were hit on the head and injured permanently? What would I do then? I might not be able to do anything.

Then there was the other side of it. I just couldn't see myself holding off from not running into a fence afraid I might be injured; or moving off the plate in the batter's box because I was afraid I might get hit in the head and be injured seriously. The responsibility of being a family man and earning a living for the family . . . all these things were going through my mind, and I just said maybe it would be best if I got out and got into something else. And I was dead serious about quitting at the time.

I know some people raised the question that I was using the retirement story as a lever to get more money. That was totally false. I've never come up with any wrinkles at contract time to try to get more money. I have always let my years speak for themselves. And why should I come up with a gimmick in 1962, when I had just had my best year in baseball? If I did have a gimmick, wouldn't it have been better to save it for when I had an off-year and needed more leverage?

Naturally, I did have trouble with Bill DeWitt over my contract for the 1962 season. In 1961 we won the pennant and I won the Most Valuable Player award and when I went in to talk contract with him he said, "I'll give you a twenty-five-hundred-dollar raise."

He must have seen me quiver because he hastily explained himself. He said, "Well, if I jump you up ten or fifteen thousand now, you'll come back next year and want twice as much. You go out and have another year like that one and you can come back and get that kind of money."

I said, "Look, it's an insult to even offer me that figure."

He was unmoved. Not that I expected him to jump up and say, okay, and offer me two or three thousand more just because I said I wouldn't sign for his figure. But he was ridiculous. You could sit for hours and he'd never move off that one figure. And you'd have four or five meetings and it would still be the same salary.

But that was Bill DeWitt. In all my dealings with him, I never had a peaceful discussion on salary. That's the way he dealt with all the players. He would come out with the cold figures on a piece of paper and never mind what a fellow had done during the summer and under what conditions he did them, when he was hurt, and things like that. He was going by the cold figures and he just stuck with them. He wouldn't move one way or the other.

It went on like that between us for four or five meetings that winter. I finally got a $12,500 raise for 1962, but I had to sweat for it. And I went through the same wringer each year with Bill DeWitt.

But it wasn't the money that made me consider retirement, it wasn't that at all. The 1962 season, so frustrating, had taken a little extra out of me. Maybe I was going a little harder than the years before. I was just beat. I was exhausted.

Personally, I was a much better ballplayer in 1962 than '61. I had a year when, after a slow start, nothing seemed to go wrong. I hit around .250 in April and most of May, but then I started hitting and never stopped. It was the kind of year when I would drive in all the runs in ball games, not one day, not two days out of the week, but three or four days in a row. I was just hitting the ball real hard and real sharp all the time. I had fifty-one doubles that year (the last time anyone had more in the National League was when Stan Musial hit fifty-three in 1953), and about twenty of them just missed being home runs. It wasn't balls going between outfielders. It was balls bouncing off the walls, missing a home run by a few inches, and winding up as doubles. I know one player doesn't win the ball game, but the opportunity was there to drive in runs and I didn't miss too many opportunities. I drove in 136 runs all told.

But we didn't win the pennant. We just weren't as consistent a ball club as we were the year before, though we did win ninety-eight games, five more than we had in 1961 when we did win the pennant.

We got off to a slow start and one reason, I think, was a severe leg fracture suffered by Gene Freese in spring training. That meant we had to juggle the infield and it took a while to get stabilized. But in August we won nine games in a row and eighteen out of twenty-one, and it looked like we might move in. But each time we'd get close we just couldn't push over the top. Although we were playing good ball, we seemed always to be playing catch-up ball. I think one mistake we made was that we always seemed to be shooting for the Dodgers. We should have been playing the team in front of us, then gone after the Dodgers. But we kept looking at the Dodgers, who had been our fiercest rivals for so many years. And, at the end of the season, it was the Giants in first place, not the Dodgers (though it took a playoff to do it), and Cincinnati in third.

I continued to enjoy myself playing against the Dodgers. I remember one late-summer game it came to the tenth inning. With one out there were men on second and third and Vada was the hitter in front of me. So manager Walt Alston had Pinson intentionally walked to load the bases and set up the double play.

Larry Sherry got two quick strikes on me. They must have looked like odd swings because afterwards people asked, "What were you trying to do, set him up? You weren't taking a real good swing." But I wasn't trying to set him up. I was just trying to meet the ball, hit a fly ball to get the run in from third. And Sherry threw me two real good sliders and I had to reach for the ball each time.

The third pitch was another slider, but it didn't break outside. Again, I was just trying to hit the ball, but this time it jumped off the bat. I didn't think it was a home run at first, but it went completely over the scoreboard, fifty-five feet up, 383 feet out.

And, as usual, a Dodger pitcher managed to hit me. This time it was Larry Sherry. If I hadn't thrown my left hand up in front of my face, I would have been hit in the head. As it was, the ball hit me on my ring finger and split the skin of the finger, and I still have the scar.

I went to first base and it was still bleeding and I kept shaking it off. It was pretty dirty, too, because I had hit the ground afterwards. I got all the way around to third base and the coach came over and looked at it and told me to get out of there.

"I'm all right," I said, "I'll get out when I score."

"You'll get out now," he said.

They called time and I retired to the clubhouse where they cleaned it up and taped it.

The next day one of the newspapermen asked me, "Isn't there a way to retaliate personally when you get thrown at like that?"

"You mean bunting down the first-base line and forcing the pitcher to cover the bag and then letting him have it?"

"Yeah, that's it," he said.

I shook my head. "There's no point in bunting for personal revenge when I can swing the bat and help the whole team." I didn't tell him what a knockdown pitch does to me, how it makes me more determined, wakes me up more (Gene Mauch, the Phillies' manager, supposedly told his pitchers one year that if they threw at me they would get fined; he didn't want to see me "aroused"). The next time up you want to get a hit off this guy, you don't want him to get you out. The last thing you want him to do is get you out. You say: He's knocked me down. I know why he's knocked me down, to get a pitch on the outside and get me to falling back on the breaking pitch. And when he does get you out, especially when he gets you out like that, you feel like he's won the ball game there. So I just go up against this type of pitcher and tell myself, I'm not going to let him win. I'm not going to let him get me out.

Aside from the normal amount of direct hits by the pitcher, I stayed pretty clear of severe injuries in 1962, though the little hurts piled up (and seemed to take longer to heal). Early in the season I fouled a ball down on my toe and it kept paining me continually when I put my weight on it and ran on it. I finally had it X-rayed and it showed a break. They just taped the bones together and I continued to play.

I got hurt another time making a catch, but that one I'll always remember. It saved the ball game.

There were one or two men on base in a late inning, the tying and winning runs I remember, and Jim Davenport was up for the Giants. Davenport always liked to move the ball around quite a bit. He could pull the ball down the left-field line, up the middle, or into right field. So I was shading a little toward the right-field line. He hit the ball to right-center and I made quite a run for it. I dove for the ball and caught it and did a somersault and tumbled over and I strained my back. But it wasn't a serious injury and I think it helped make me a better hitter that year. I wasn't able to turn as much at bat and I think it made me concentrate more on hitting the ball sharply.

And I did hit sharply. In addition to leading the league in doubles, I led in runs scored with 134. I got 208 hits, the most I've ever gotten in a single year. I hit thirty-nine home runs and stole eighteen bases and batted .342, just four points less than the league-leader, Tommy Davis.

Davis had a terrific year for the Dodgers and I felt sure that he would win the Most Valuable Player award for 1963. But he didn't win it; his teammate, Maury Wills, did.

I really felt this was an injustice. Tommy won the batting title, he hit twenty-seven home runs, only twenty-seven homers, yet he drove in 156 runs! But they chose Maury Wills, who set the stolen-base record that year with 104. They said, "Wills gets on all the time, he's on second and third and Davis drives him in." Well, sure he's on second and third all the time, but someone still has to drive him in, and if Davis doesn't drive him in he doesn't score. How many times did Wills steal home? None. So someone had to drive him in. I think you've got to go quite a way back to find someone who did what Davis did and not be named MVP. I don't know if any player will ever have another year like that, what with today's baseball, the platoon, the relief pitching, the era of the specialist.

In July and August we won forty-three games and lost twenty and yet we couldn't climb into first place. Then, in September, we tailed off, winning sixteen, losing twelve, and falling out of the pennant race. And that, for me, was the

worst blow of all and made up my mind about quitting baseball.

After the news of my retirement broke, I found it very difficult to get anyone to believe me. Mr. DeWitt, for one, was
very cool. "Robinson's over twenty-one," he said, "he's got
a mind of his own and he can do what he wants to."

Gene Mauch, who was managing the Phillies, seemed to
take it very well. He told a writer, "I know ninety-one pitchers
in the league and nine managers who will chip in five hundred
dollars apiece if Robinson will go through with his plans to
retire. That's fifty thousand dollars."

But the loosest group of all was my teammates. Before
our final game, manager Fred Hutchinson called a clubhouse
meeting.

"I see where this is the last game for one of us," Hutch
said, "and I think we all should say an appropriate farewell
to our boy, Robby." One by one, the players came over and
shook my hands, all very solemn. The last one was Eddie
Kasko, with a package.

"We just want you to know," Eddie said, "how much we're
going to miss you. And as a token of our esteem, we have a
gift we're sure you'll be able to use in your new job." He
unwrapped the thing, handing me a beat-up old lunch pail.

We were playing the Cardinals that afternoon and when
I went up to the plate in the seventh inning, the Cincinnati
organist played "Auld Lang Syne." It was a put-up job because my teammates stood at attention in the dugout, their
caps covering their hearts.

What could I do for such nice guys? I hit a double, my
fifty-first of the season.

And, after the game, I went over to manager Hutchinson
and casually mentioned to him that I'd see him in the spring.

I still thought I would retire, I was still very serious about
it, but I was cooling off. And after I had a winter in which to
reflect, and after I got my strength back, I knew I just
couldn't get out of the game. It was too much a part of me.

Which brings up a point. When it finally does come time for me to quit playing, will I truly be able to? The answer is, I don't know. I try to tell myself nowadays that when it comes time for me to get out, I'll know it and be able to do it and won't try to hang on. But will I? Every athlete says he'll know when it's time to quit, and when that time comes, he'll quit. But that's quite a decision to make, to just say—well, that's it. And I admire the ones who are able to do it. Of course I would rather go out on top than hang around too long. But whether I'll be able to do it or not is another thing. I don't know. But I hope I don't have to make that decision for a few more years.

13 What Is a Clique?

Maybe I should have retired after all, because when I started to talk contract for the 1963 season with general manager Bill DeWitt, I was offered a raise of twenty-five hundred dollars.

I was kind of shocked about that, since I had come off the greatest year of my career, and of course I told Mr. DeWitt, nothing doing.

This went back and forth for a while, as it always did when you discussed salary with Bill DeWitt, and finally I got what I felt was a satisfactory raise—$22,500, plus options depending on attendance and things like that.

And then I went out and had the worst year of my career.

Looking back at 1963, I still shudder. It was a nightmare. My previous bad season, 1958, was nothing like it. That year I got hit on the head and it took me a half-year to untrack. But that was the only injury. In 1963 I started off fast, and then went downhill. It was nothing but injuries all season long, one piled up on another. I don't think there was one game when I was 100 percent.

First it was a sore shoulder, then an inflamed elbow, which meant I wasn't able to throw real good from the outfield. Then I got hit on the fist with an inside pitch and I jammed my thumb. Then it was a muscle pull in the back of my leg, which lingered on and on. Finally, on September 7, it was all capped by a collision at second base with Ron Hunt of the Mets. He came down on my arm and it required thirty stitches to close the wound and they said I was through for the season.

Ten days later I was back playing. The thing was, we had

a shot at third place, which meant extra money for all of us, and I thought I might be able to help out. My arm wasn't right, of course; when I tried to straighten the arm completely, I could feel it pulling on the muscle. But I bent my forearm when I hit, so I was able to maneuver the arm well enough to swing a bat.

But I didn't do much for the ball club down the stretch, and I thought about that for a long time.

We were playing St. Louis the last three games of the season. The Cardinals had second place all to themselves but we had to beat them in all three games to have any chance to catch Philadelphia and San Francisco. The Phillies were playing the pennant-winning Dodgers and the Giants were playing Pittsburgh.

Well, we won our first two games from the Cardinals, even though I went zero-for-eight. Pittsburgh and the Giants split their two games, and the Phillies took two straight from the Dodgers. That left the Giants a game ahead in third place and the Phillies tied with us for fourth.

On Sunday, the last game of the season, the Giants won to clinch third place, the Phillies won their third straight from the Dodgers and they took fourth place because we went fourteen innings with the Cardinals and finally lost, 3–2. And I remember two things about that game: Stan Musial ended his tremendous career by getting two hits and driving in one run; and I ended the season with no hits in six at-bats. And I always said, if I hadn't been in there, if I hadn't come back, somebody else might have gone in and been able to do the job and there would have been a little more money for the rest of the fellas. And that has always bothered me, and even today I am full of regret over that season and especially over the way it ended.

But I can't blame my showing—I batted .259, with twenty-one home runs and ninety-one runs-batted-in—all on injuries. A lot of things were happening to me that year that had never happened to me before.

On the field, maybe because of the injuries, I was pressing an awful lot. I stole twenty-six bases, which is my personal season's high, but I was taking a lot more chances than I should have. With the muscle pull I wasn't able to run as fast as normal, yet I tried to play as I always did. When I got on first base I tried to steal a base, and many times I got thrown out because I wasn't moving fast enough. And there were times when I got picked off first because I was trying to take a little bigger lead and I couldn't get back to the bag fast enough. And my hitting was affected, too. I wasn't doing things naturally. I was out there trying too hard and as a result I made a lot of mistakes that I wouldn't ordinarily make.

I also had a run-in with my manager that was at least partly my fault, and got me down for quite a while.

This was about the end of June. I had been bothered by a groin injury, and then I strained my wrist checking a swing. We were in San Francisco at the time and we weren't going too well and, after a losing game, I passed by manager Freddy Hutchinson's locker and he stopped me.

He said, "How's the wrist?"

"Not too good," I said.

"Well, is it bothering your swing?"

"Yes, it is, to a certain extent."

"Well, we'll rest you tomorrow and rest you in the Houston series. Get the thing healed up because I want you back in that lineup."

I said, "Fine, if that's what you want."

So I sat out the one game left in San Francisco, and I sat out two more in Houston and I was sitting out the third game, on a Sunday, when we had the bases loaded, nobody out, and we needed a pinch-hitter.

By this time I felt I could play, but no one had even asked me, you know, are you all right, are you ready to play. I didn't think it was my place to go up to anyone and say, I'm ready to go. It was the wrong way of thinking on my part, but that's the way I felt at the time.

So I was sitting on the bench and now he wants a pinch-hitter. He walked up and down on the bench. He walked right past me without even looking. Finally, he called in catcher Don Pavletich from the bullpen to come in and pinch-hit. And Pavletich hit into a double play and Houston got out of the inning without a run being scored and we went on to lose the game.

And I was burning. Heck, I might have gone up and done the same thing as Pavletich, but the fact that the manager didn't even ask me if I could pinch-hit really got under my skin.

The next day a local reporter came around before the game and asked me how my hand was. I told him it was fine. He asked me if I could play. I told him, yes, I can play.

"Then why in the world aren't you playing?" he asked, exasperated. "Haven't you told the manager that you can play?"

"No," I said.

"Why?" he asked.

"Because the manager hasn't asked me." I admit that sounds terribly childish in cold print, but you have to understand how much my pride was hurt. The manager took me out of the lineup and he didn't tell me to tell him when I was ready to go back in. I expected him to come over and at least ask me if I was ready. But he never did. I didn't understand then that it just might have been an oversight on his part, that he had twenty-four other guys to look after and he couldn't get involved with one individual. You get wrapped up in so many other things and you just forget a little thing like that. So I guess it was my place to have gone to him and told him that I was ready to play.

Anyway, that interview hit the papers in Cincinnati and created a little stir. The front office called Hutch in Houston, and Bill DeWitt asked him what was going on, and then Hutch called me in and talked to me about it.

"Did you say what appeared in the paper?" he asked.

I said, "Yes, I said it."

Then we had a little discussion, if that's what you want to call it. When the Bear engaged in such "discussions," you never forgot them. But we finally did come to an understanding. I assured him there were no ill-feelings on my part, that I had just been disappointed when he hadn't asked me if I could pinch-hit, that I thought I might have helped the ball club at the time.

So I got back in the starting lineup and it was all straightened out, but I don't think Bill DeWitt ever forgot that. And one reason why I am now playing for Baltimore might be traced to that little incident in 1963; that might have been the beginning of the whole cycle.

But there were other things, too. It was 1963 when the talk first started that Vada Pinson and I had formed a "Negro clique" on the ball club. One New York sports columnist wrote, "They say the two have formed a clique that is gnawing at the morale of the club and that's why the Reds are finishing sixth instead of fighting for the flag."

That's all the writer really said. He didn't say what he meant by a clique, and he didn't say who "they" were, except to infer that it was people close to the club. "*They* [italics mine] call it, simply, 'the situation,' and they say something will have to be done about it."

Now that was a dandy statement. The situation. Did the writer talk to any of the white players on the club then? Did he talk to any of the Negro players? I know if he did, he didn't talk to me about it.

The truth is, there was no clique on that team, no more than there is a clique on any team in baseball. On every ball club you have fellows who have a lot in common and who like to do things together. Under the unwritten rules of baseball in those days (it's not as bad now) the Negro players and the white players were friends *on* the field, but once the game was over, went their separate ways. There were always two or three white players on the Reds (on any team for that matter) who went together on the road—to the movies, clubs, or wherever they wanted to go. And nothing was ever said about them having a clique.

In fact, Vada and I were never really invited to go along with these fellows. So we went our own way. We usually went back to the hotel after a night game and had a sandwich or snack in the room and watched television for a couple of hours before we went to bed. During the day, we'd get up and have breakfast sent up, relax a little bit, and then maybe go to a movie. Or if I wanted to see a particular movie and Vada didn't, I'd go and he'd do whatever he wanted.

I could never understand why they picked the two of us out to say we had a clique going. They always talked about cliques being among Negro players, or Latin players, seldom about the white players. Naturally, Negro ballplayers are thrown together. With four or five on the ball club, you're going to be together. With fifteen or twenty white players naturally there's a chance to switch off a little bit, but they had their "cliques," too, if that's what you want to call it.

Remember the Yankees of the late 1950s and early '60s? Whitey Ford and Mickey Mantle and Yogi Berra mostly hung together. Then there was a group made up of Bobby Richardson and Tony Kubek, the "milkshake drinkers," they called them. But I don't think they ever referred to either group as a clique.

At any rate, no one on the ball club ever said anything directly to me about a clique—not the management, the manager, or the players. And I never had any real harsh words or arguments with anyone about things like that.

The clique thing was just nonsense. I suppose if Vada and I weren't so close, they might have started calling me a "loner," and blaming that on the decline of the ball club. Either way I probably would have gotten it. In a baseball game there's always a winner or a loser but in your own life it's sometimes hard to tell whether you've won or lost, or whether you've even been in the game.

Still the clique talk grew and grew. Vada and I were referred to as "self-appointed Negro leaders." One magazine carried a headline: Frank Robinson-Vada Pinson: DOUBLE TROUBLE. The article then went on to say absolutely nothing to back up that headline, but that's how the thing kept building up, until the clique business became a fact to many people, became established in people's minds.

Naturally, my off-year in 1963 intensified that talk, although Vada didn't have an off-year. Not at all. He batted .313, led the league in hits and triples, drove in 106 runs, and had one of his best years ever. So our "clique" apparently didn't hurt his performance.

Yet, with all that was going on, with what was happening to me on the field, with what was being whispered off the field, I began to get down on myself. It wasn't just the idea that I was having a bad year. The ball club was having a bad year, and I felt that I wasn't doing my job.

My opinion, unhappily, was quickly reinforced by the front office. Bill DeWitt started negotiating my salary in public midway in 1963 when he made a lot of statements about my failure to drive in *the big run*. He said something to the effect that, "When we're winning 11–2, Robinson will knock in seven runs. When we're losing, he doesn't get a hit." If that was his thinking, fine. He made it clear what he thought of me as a ballplayer. But was it necessarily true? I don't think so. I don't care if you only drive in twenty runs a year, some of those runs have to help win ball games, set up situations. And I was averaging a hundred RBIs a year, so some of them had to be in 2–1 and 3–2 ball games where they certainly meant something.

But he had the figures going with him in 1963 and I took a cut in salary, a bad cut. It was such a bad cut, I told a writer later, "that I'm going to drop over the Reds' office and have the stitches taken out."

Laughing on the outside. The cut wasn't 25 percent, the maximum they can inflict on you, but it was bad enough. It was the first cut I'd taken in my baseball career and I felt it was uncalled for. But all they do is look at the figures. When they're getting ready to cut you, they look at the bare figures, and when the figures are good and you've got a raise coming, they look at other things. But that's baseball.

By this time, Mr. DeWitt was really getting to me. It wasn't just the salary negotiations. You expect that in baseball, because these general managers are all businessmen; they're trying to make the best possible deal for their ball club. It was more than money that came between the two of us.

In my early years with Cincinnati, I had really kept my feelings to myself. I was young and a loner and I didn't think it was right to speak out about things that bothered me, or maybe it was because I didn't know how to go about it. But in my later years with Cincinnati—I would say from 1961 on—I did start to speak out more and I continued to speak out for what I thought was right. And in those years, as I became the oldest player in point of service on the ball club, the other players began taking their troubles to me. I would present them to the manager as *my* troubles— I never went over the manager's head—and if the manager told me to go to the front office with them, that's what I did. And I got labeled as a troublemaker because of this. And I guess I was a troublemaker if it meant standing up and speaking my piece when I thought I was right.

There was one spring when we were scheduled to play a three-game exhibition series in Mexico City. The squad was divided in two, with half the players going to Mexico, the other half staying behind in Tampa. To save money, management told those players who were staying in Tampa that they would have to double up with someone else, and the ones who were going would have to pack up all their clothes

and put them in a storeroom at our hotel in Tampa, the
Causeway Inn.

Well, the players just didn't want to go through all of this.
Why couldn't everything be left the way it was? And they
came to me with this problem, and I took it to the manager
as my problem.

I happened to be going to Mexico City and Vada was staying behind. I told the manager I didn't want to pack all my
clothes and put them in a storage room and have to come
back and take them all out and have them pressed and
cleaned and things like that when I got back.

Well, they thought I was griping about myself. They said,
"Okay, you can leave your clothes in your room, and Pinson
can stay in his room." But the other fellows would still have
to move their clothes and double up. I didn't think that was
fair and I told them so and finally everyone got the same deal
that they gave me.

That was being a troublemaker. I was such a troublemaker
that one winter I was called into the Reds' front office and
told: "All the young players look up to you. We want you to
go out there and be a team leader."

And yet, after I was traded to Baltimore, when a writer
suggested to Mr. DeWitt that some of the Reds' players
would miss me for my "leadership qualities," he said he felt
that Johnny Edwards was more of a team leader than I was.

That was fine with me. I never claimed to be the team
leader. I just went out and played a certain brand of baseball—good, hard baseball—and maybe a lot of the fellows
tried a little harder because they saw me doing certain things.
If they did put out a little extra because they felt I was putting
out a little bit, that was great. That's the idea, to win ball
games. But I never claimed to be the team leader in Cincinnati, and when it came down to talking contract they
never mentioned that. If Bill DeWitt felt that Johnny
Edwards, who was the Cincinnati player representative when
I was there in the last few years, was more of a team leader,

he was entitled to his opinion. I think you might have gotten a different opinion from the players themselves.

What Mr. DeWitt was trying to do in those days was work it between the two of us. He had Johnny Edwards as the leader of the white players and I was made the leader, the representative, of the Negro players. I didn't realize this until it was too late and then I was in it too deep to back out. But when it did dawn on me, I didn't like it, I didn't like it at all. For one, it helped perpetuate this myth of a "clique" among the Negro players on the ball club. For another, a team leader should be the leader of *all* the players, and if I had to do it over, I would never have fallen into that trap.

But that's what they had me do in those days. For example, Fred Hutchinson (and, later, his successor, Dick Sisler) asked me to look after Leo Cardenas. Cardenas is a Cuban Negro and they always seemed to think he was hotheaded and he didn't perform well when he got mad. And, really, it was just the idea that things weren't always explained to him. He didn't understand English well and he got confused.

Let's say there was an affair in Cincinnati and they wanted the club to be represented by a certain number of players. They would be talking in English and he wouldn't understand and no one ever took the time to explain it to him. So he would raise his hand and when the time came to go to this affair Chico would say, no, he wasn't going. And they would say, well, you held up your hand and said you were going. He said, well, I didn't understand it. So that didn't sit too well, and I tried to kind of guide him and look after him.

And I went into the 1964 season determined to have a good year and get my cut restored. And I did have a good year. I hit .306, I drove in ninety-six runs, I hit twenty-nine runs. And when I went into my negotiations for the 1965 season I asked for my full cut back, and they wouldn't do it. We had quite a debate on that, and I didn't sign until about a week before spring training, and then I only got about half of my cut back.

That 1964 season was probably the strangest of my life, strange in many ways, and tempestuous, too. For one thing, the only time I ever went after a pitcher happened in 1964.

We were playing the Giants in a series at San Francisco and in the first game, a night game, I strained my back hitting the bag hard at first base.

After the game, I was supplied with pain pills and sleeping pills and told to go right back to the hotel, gulp them all down, and sleep it off. Which is what I did. But before I fell off, I left a call with the switchboard operator to wake me at nine the next morning, because we were playing a day game.

The next morning came and I remember the phone ringing and the operator telling me what time it was, but that's all I remember. The next thing I know there's a pounding at the door. It's the bellboy.

"You're due at the ball park, Mr. Robinson," he says.

"What time is it?"

"It's eleven-thirty."

"Oh, boy." I somehow got myself together and took a cab to the ball park and arrived there about forty-five minutes before game time.

But I was still groggy because the pills hadn't worn off, and my back was bothering me. I went in and they put some heat on my back and then I took a cold shower. I went out on the field about five minutes to one and tried to make small talk in the dugout to wake myself up, but it was a strain.

"Can you play?" the manager asked.

"I guess so," I said. "I'm here."

Ron Herbel was pitching for the Giants, and our first three hitters up got hits. I was the fourth hitter and, on the first pitch, Herbel drilled me on the left elbow.

There's no doubt in my mind that he was throwing at me and I became more aroused than I had ever been. I started to the mound after him. I don't think I would have done it—

[5] I got hit in the arm in this game against the San Francisco Giants in 1961, the year we won the pennant. It could have been worse—it could have been the head. In six of my ten years in the National League I led the league in being hit by the pitcher. (Photograph by Wide World.)

[6] Here I am sliding into home plate against the Braves as Hank Aaron's throw from right field arrives too late. I've always slid like that, ever since I was a boy raising strawberries on my backside on the asphalt playgrounds that passed for diamonds in my ghetto neighborhood. It all comes from not wanting to lose. I do not like to lose. In fact, I cannot stand to lose. (Photograph by Wide World.)

[7] In the year of the Triple Crown, 1966, I batted .316 for the Orioles, hit forty-nine home runs, drove in 122 runs. But one of the happiest moments of my life came the night we clinched the American League pennant. (Photograph by *Sport Magazine*.)

[8] The culmination of my greatest year as a ballplayer, when I was awarded a sports car for being the most valuable player in the 1966 World Series against the Dodgers. I was especially happy that my wife, Barbara, could share the moment with me. (Photograph by *Sport Magazine*.)

oh, I *know* I wouldn't because I never did it before and never have since—but the back was paining and I was still half asleep.

With the help of some peacemakers, I was stopped half-way to the mound. A few words were said and I went on to first base. Then the jockeying began from the Giant bench. Leading the jeering section was Gaylord Perry. I couldn't distinguish what he was saying but I knew he was on me. He was standing so I would be sure to see him, and he was going at it pretty good.

I hollered over to him, "Wait till tomorrow. You'll be pitching."

He said, "Tomorrow, I stick one in your ear."

I said, "Well, you'll have your chance."

The next batter hit a ground ball to the shortstop and I went in pretty hard and flipped the second baseman, Chuck Hiller. He actually fell over and I hit him in the chest, and we got tangled up pretty good. I guess he was a little angry because he started to kind of flip me and I told him to take it easy and let me go.

I started back to the dugout and Jim Davenport, who was playing third base, said, "What are you trying to prove?"

I said, "I'm not trying to prove anything. What are you guys trying to prove?"

I went on to hit two home runs in that game, which we won big, and the next day, my first time up, I hit a home run off Gaylord Perry.

At the time of this incident, Dick Sisler had taken over as manager of the Reds. Fred Hutchinson was ill, very ill with cancer, and this had a profound effect on the ball club.

The news of his illness became public after the 1963 season, when he had to undergo special cobalt treatment. Then, a few times during the early part of the season, he had to leave the ball club for further treatment.

And when he came back you could look at the man and tell he was real sick. You could see it in his face, in the movement of his body, in his stiffness as he walked. Everybody tried to ignore the fact and not talk about it too much, but it was in all our minds. In fact we might have been just a little tense, a little too tight because of his illness. I think we were more conscious of making mistakes, that if we did make a mistake on the field we would intensify his pain, his agony. And we might have tried a little too hard to win for Hutch.

Finally, he had to give it up and coach Dick Sisler took over. Dick was a fine manager and a fine man but we did miss Hutch. I didn't always get along with him but in the later years I began to understand him more and come to learn that beneath his gruff exterior was a kind, gentle man. And of course we all admired his courage, in the way he was fighting this thing.

He only came to see us once after he left the ball club. It was the last week of the season when we had just come off the road and still had a good chance at the National League pennant.

He came into the clubhouse looking shrunken and very old, hardly able to talk. We were shocked and saddened by his appearance. He slumped on a chair and said to us, in a whisper—"I don't want you to win it for me, I want you to win it for yourself."

I was in Cincinnati on November 12 of that year when I heard the news of his death on television. And it was a shock even though I knew it was coming. Death always comes as a shock, especially when it comes to someone who is close to you. Losing Hutch was like losing a member of the family. And his death stunned me for a while.

And it was too bad that we couldn't have won that 1964 pennant for Hutch—or for ourselves, as he would have wanted—but in the fading weeks of that season we came as close as you can get.

With two weeks to go we were five and a half games behind the Phillies. Then we went on and swept a three-game series in Philadelphia and a five-game series in New York. The

Phillies kept losing—they lost ten in a row—and, suddenly, we were in first place by a game with five to play.

But we lost two out of three to the Pirates, and we dropped a half-game behind the Cardinals.

On the final Friday night of the season we were playing the Phillies at home.

It turned out to be one of the most frustrating games I can ever remember.

Jimmy O'Toole was pitching and doing a great job as he had all year. He won seventeen games for us, and in this one he had a 3–0 lead going into the seventh inning.

In our half of the seventh, Chris Short, the Phils' pitcher, hit Chico Cardenas with a pitch. Chico didn't like it at all. In fact, he was enraged. He held onto his bat and started toward the mound, hollering, "I'm going to hit you with the bat."

Well, everyone ran out on the field and there was a lot of pushing and shoving, but nothing happened.

And we held that 3–0 lead going into the eighth, and Frank Thomas came up to pinch-hit for the Phils. O'Toole hit him on the fists and Thomas hit a little pop fly right over second base. Pete Rose was playing second and Chico was playing shortstop and they both started after the ball and neither one of them called for it. They both stopped and the ball dropped in and the Phillies went on to score four runs and they beat us 4–3.

After the game everyone was in the clubhouse and O'Toole came after Cardenas. He said Chico had cost him the ball game, that he should have caught the ball. And, as I said, Chico didn't really understand English in those days and he didn't understand everything that was said. So one thing led to another and they started at one another and it was broken up.

This was in the trainer's room. O'Toole walked back in the clubhouse and then Cardenas walked in. There is a little table in the clubhouse where they keep wire brushes and things to clean your shoes, and on the table was an ice pick. Cardenas picked it up. O'Toole was at one end of the room and Cardenas was at the other and Chico picked up the ice pick and started for Jim.

"You say I miss ball," he hollered, "I get you." I jumped in and stopped Chico, and some of the other players helped.

"Put it down, Chico," I said, "put it down." And I took the ice pick away from him. And they never got within fifty feet of each other. It was an unfortunate incident, a classic case of misunderstanding. Cardenas was naturally at fault for losing his temper and picking up that ice pick, and O'Toole was at fault for blaming Chico for losing the ball game. But you have to remember, this game meant so much to us and the tension was very high and tempers just flared. We all lost the ball game, not just Cardenas and not just O'Toole. We had come that far as a ball club, we had won games as a ball club, and we had lost games as a ball club, but no one individual should be blamed for any loss.

On the final day of the season we were tied with the Cardinals, and a game ahead of the Phillies. If we beat the Phillies and the Cards lost, we win the pennant. If we win and the Cards win, we'd still be tied with them.

It wasn't to be. The Phils beat us 12–0 and we were never in the ball game.

When it was over we went into the clubhouse and listened to the radio, listened to the Cardinals as they took the Mets apart.

"Maybe the Mets will rally," someone said forlornly.

"We can't expect any help now," I said. "We had a chance to do it ourselves and we missed it."

The Cards beat the Mets and won the pennant, and I sat there by my locker, head down, unable to move. So close, so close, I said to myself. So close, and we come up empty. It was a long time before I could pick myself up, shower, get into my street clothes and leave that dressing room and the long 1964 season behind me.

14 "Well, We've Been Traded"

Late in the afternoon of December 9, 1965, I was just sitting down to dinner when the phone rang. I was eating dinner early because it was bowling night and the league started at six-thirty. But when I got off the phone I ate no dinner, and neither did my wife. The only one who ate that night was my little boy, Kevin.

The call was from Rose, the switchboard operator in the Reds' office. She asked Barbara, who had answered the phone, whether I was home. I got on the phone.

"Frank," Rose said, "Mr. Seghi would like to speak to you." Phil Seghi was the assistant general manager of the Reds. He would often call me on various matters so I thought nothing of it. But his first words rocked me.

"Frank," he said, "you've been traded to Baltimore." I said nothing. My mind went blank.

He continued, "I wanted to let you know before we release it to the papers at four-thirty."

I looked at my watch. It was four-twenty, a time I'll never forget. He was saying, "I want you to know what a great job you've done for the ball club over the years." He went on like that for a while until, finally, I recovered my voice.

"Well," I said, "who'd you get for me?" It was all I could think of saying.

"Pappas, Jack Baldschun, and Dick Simpson."

"Okay," I said.

"Good luck," he said.

"Thank you," I said, and I hung up.

Barbara hadn't been listening to the conversation but she

took one look at me and knew something had happened. "Who was that on the phone?" she asked warily.

"Mr. Seghi," I said.

"Well, what did he want?"

"Nothing."

She said, "You're not looking like that for nothing. What did he want?"

I said, "Well, we've been traded."

She said, "Whom to?"

"Baltimore."

"Who?"

"Baltimore."

There was a slight pause, then she said, "Oh, well, it could have been worse."

At that moment, I was quite sure nothing could have been worse. I was physically shaken. Immediately, I asked myself, why? I knew it could happen. In fact, earlier in the winter I felt sure that it *would* happen. But then all the talk died down, and now this hit me unexpectedly. And I just asked myself—why? why? And I was shocked, and I was hurt.

Actually, at the end of the 1965 season, I felt that there would be quite a bit of trading on the ball club. We had come close to a pennant in 1964 and just missed out. And we were picked again to win it in 1965. We stayed in the pennant race until the last week of the season. And we fell flat on our face and wound up fourth.

When a club collapses like that—from fighting for the top spot in a week to finishing fourth—something's got to give.

The first thing to give, naturally, was the manager. Dick Sisler was fired right after the season, and I felt that was an injustice. I think Sisler did an outstanding job under the circumstances. He couldn't foresee that Jimmy O'Toole was going to have a bad year, that Joey Jay wasn't going to win the way you knew he could. But the players were happy with Sisler, with the job he was doing, and gave 100 percent at all

times. I just don't think the front office was ever happy with
Sisler. I don't think they wanted to hire him in the first place
after he took over as acting manager for Freddy Hutchinson,
who had become seriously ill. Sisler did a fine job in '64 and
I think they felt compelled to hire him for '65 after Hutch
passed away. They gave him a one-year contract. But I think
they were just looking for an out, to find a way to fire him.
And what better way than when we wound up fourth after
being so close all season long? That was their opportunity
and they grabbed it.

And all season long the front office kept meddling in his
affairs as a manager, kept interfering with him. I remember
one incident toward the close of the season. We were scheduled for a doubleheader and Chico Cardenas played the first
game and then he told Dick Sisler he couldn't play the second
game. So Dick came to me and said, "Chico isn't playing the
second game. I'm putting Helms in."

I asked him why (this was when I was supposed to be
looking after Chico, at Dick's request). He said, "He says
he has an eye infection."

I said, "Before you make the change, let me talk to him."

Cardenas was in a slump and I wanted to make sure he
just wasn't down on himself and using an excuse not to play.

I went over to Chico and I said, "What's wrong?"

He said, "My eye's bothering me."

"If there's any way you can go out there," I said, "you
should go out there and play. But if the eye is really bothering
you bad, you shouldn't go." I made a point of saying, "Don't
let anything personal, anything you're mad about ever affect
your play on the field." I said, "Just because you might be
mad or may not be hitting well, you mustn't let that interfere with your playing." He assured me his eye was really
bothering him, so I went back to Dick Sisler and I told him
that Chico did have the bad eye.

Tommy Helms went in at shortstop and he played about a
week and he did a great job. Then Chico recovered, and even

though Helms was doing so well, Sisler decided to put Chico back in the lineup. That didn't sit well with the front office. Not at all. But Sisler said, "Cardenas has brought me this far and he's my starting shortstop." Dick just felt he wanted his best in there and Cardenas was the best shortstop in the National League in 1965, so he defied the front office and put Chico back in. And they didn't like that one bit.

With a few breaks, though, we might have gone all the way in 1965, and Dick Sisler might still be managing the Cincinnati ball club, and I might still be playing for Cincinnati. But it was the kind of a season we could never put anything together as a ball club, and that certainly was no fault of Sisler's. One thing for sure, we might have gotten more help from the front office. Our bullpen, for instance, was in dreadful shape.

In 1964 Sammy Ellis and Billy McCool worked the bullpen and they gave us an outstanding left-right combination. In fact they almost pitched us to the pennant coming out of the bullpen in 1964. But in 1965 they made Ellis a starter and the load fell completely on McCool. He was just a kid, only twenty years old, and he did a fine job, but he couldn't do it alone. Gerry Arrigo was in the bullpen and he didn't do a thing. Roger Craig was in the bullpen and he didn't do a thing. Jim Duffalo was down there and didn't do a thing. These fellows stayed with us until July and then the front office made a move to strengthen the bullpen. They brought in a kid, Ted Davidson, and a veteran, Dom Zanni, from San Diego. They did a good job for us right away and the ball club started to move. I think if the front office had made the move a little sooner we probably would have won the pennant.

As it was, every time we looked like we were ready to go, we'd drop a tough ball game. A home run or a big base hit would beat us. We never won more than four games in a row all season long. Each time we'd win four and be leading in the fifth ball game, against ball clubs like Houston, the Mets, ball clubs you should beat, something bad would happen.

I remember a doubleheader at Crosley Field late in the season against Houston. We went into it with four straight victories, only 3½ games out of first.

We started out great. I hit a three-run homer and we had a 6–4 lead going into the eighth. Then they brought in Jim Gentile to pinch-hit. He was batting about .200 at the time, but he came up and hit a three-run home run. And that beat us.

The last week of the season we went to Houston for a three-game series. We won the first two games and were just three behind the Dodgers. Our next stop was Dodger Stadium. If we could beat Houston in this third game, and if the Dodgers lost, that would put us only two behind going into a three-game series with the Dodgers.

Well, we led 2–1 in the ninth inning. Then Joe Morgan led off with a single and Lee Maye forced Morgan and Jimmy Wynn walked. That brought up Chuck Harrison, who nobody knew of at the time—he had just been recalled from Oklahoma City. And, wouldn't you know? Harrison hit his first major-league home run off us and that was the ball game.

So instead of going out to play the Dodgers two games back, we were three back. We knew we had to take the three-game series to even seriously challenge them. So they threw Podres at us in the first game and he and Ron Perranoski beat us. And we lost the next two ball games and that knocked us right out of the pennant race. And that's the way it went all year long. As soon as we got to that big ball game, the one ball game that would put us over the hump, we would drop it.

So we just felt there was going to be some trading, and I felt that I would quite possibly be one of the ones to be traded.

It was a combination of things that made me feel that way. Bill DeWitt was now the owner of the ball club and he had made it pretty clear what he thought of me. We had some good-looking kids sitting on the bench, and I felt he would much rather trade off an older fellow, one he felt might have only two or three years left, to make room for the youngster with potential. And I felt that older fellow who might go was me.

DeWitt had plenty of ammunition, too, in 1965. I was booed badly throughout the year by the home folks. There was one streak in particular when I went zero for twenty-two that the fans really got on me. That bothered me quite a bit. I don't think any player in baseball, or in any sport, can say that booing doesn't bother him. Maybe if it happens only on occasions, it won't. But if it goes on continuously, as it did in Cincinnati when I was in that slump, it has to bother an individual, and it did bother me. I tried not to let it, I tried to fight it as best I could. I tried to keep my composure and self-control and not blow up. I just tried to battle my way out of the slump. That was the main thing because I knew as soon as I started hitting they would all be on my side again. But I didn't feel too good about being booed, not only because I was down, but because I had been in Cincinnati for nine years and the fans knew exactly what I could do and I thought maybe they should be a little bit more tolerant. But maybe I wasn't being fair to them. Maybe they expected too much of me or maybe they deserved better from me. Maybe I did deserve to be booed the way I was going. I accepted it, but it did bother me. It bothered me that the home fans were booing me.

I remember one doubleheader in June when I happened to leave a couple of men stranded on base. I was booed so robustly that one visiting writer wrote, "I had to look around to see whether Mao Tse-tung had just wandered in from the bullpen." It got so bad in this period that Dick Sisler put a plea in the paper. "Don't boo him," Dick said, "boo me."

The local papers got on me, too. One columnist turned over his space every week to the fans and they always had something critical, something nasty to say about me—trade Frank Robinson, ship him out of town, etc. This same columnist, incidentally, started a campaign after I was traded to retire my number. Such are the ways of the world. Anyway, I think maybe Mr. DeWitt felt this was a chance to trade me and there wouldn't be too much pressure on him for doing it.

But the 1965 season wasn't a complete fiasco for me. I did drive in 113 runs, and anytime you drive in over a hundred runs, *some* of them must be big runs. I also hit thirty-three home runs, and batted .296. Naturally, when I don't hit over .300 I'm not happy with the year. But I felt it hadn't been a bad year, just not outstanding.

The trade talk really flew that winter. They had me going to the Yankees, they had me going to Cleveland, they had me going to Houston and Philadelphia. I do know Mr. DeWitt tried very hard to trade me to Houston. He asked for Jimmy Wynn, a fine young outfielder, and Larry Dierker, a promising young pitcher. I think Mr. DeWitt would have liked that trade, but Houston turned it down. Then Houston offered Dick Farrell, a relief pitcher who is a year older than me, and Mr. DeWitt turned that down. If anyone had asked me my preference (can't you just picture that: Mr. DeWitt coming to me and saying, "Frank, we're gonna trade you. Just tell me where you want to go.") I would have traded me to the Yankees or Indians.

I liked the Yankees because they always had an outstanding ball club, they always seemed to be in the pennant race. And I always had the desire to play in New York for a chance to make money outside of baseball, for endorsements, and TV appearances and things like that. There was never much of that in Cincinnati.

The reason I liked Cleveland was because Gabe Paul was the general manager and Birdie Tebbetts was the manager, and they were my bosses when I broke into the majors. I knew

that they knew what I could do as a ballplayer and that if I
went to Cleveland, there would be less pressure on me.

In any case, my name kept popping up every day. Any time
you see a name mentioned in trades as often as mine was in
this period, you just feel there has to be some fire somewhere. During the winter league meetings, the complete week
of that meeting, my name was in the papers every day, going
to one ball club or another.

But then the meetings ended. No trade. Nothing. The
talk died out completely. So I felt that maybe I had escaped,
and I adjusted my thinking. And just when I was reconciled
to playing with Cincinnati in 1966, the trade was made. I
was back in the pit.

I did go bowling the night of December 9. Barbara tried
to talk me out of it but I wanted to go out and say goodbye
to my friends. I also wanted to get away from the telephone.
The one call I did take was from Vada Pinson. He got on the
phone and said, "Roomie, what are they trying to do?"

I said, "They done it." We had a little discussion and
then I got away from the phone. I knew the reporters would
be calling and I wasn't ready to speak with them. I thought
I might say something I would be sorry for later. I wanted
to give myself time to think things out a little bit, pull myself together. So I went bowling and I bowled very badly and
I thought about my future.

The thing is, I had begun to feel that Cincinnati would be
part of that future. Anytime you spend ten years in someone's company you just feel comfortable and hope that you
can continue on the same way. When I first made it to the
majors, my one thought was: I want to get in ten years. At
the time, though, I certainly wasn't thinking too much of ten
years with one ball club. I just felt I would be fortunate to
get ten years in—period. Then as the years went by and,
finally, I did have ten years with the same organization, I
began thinking of a future tied up with that organization.

I thought I might finish my playing career with the Reds and maybe some day get a coaching job with them . . . maybe even someday manage in Cincinnati.

Now that was all over with. Now I had to look ahead. I did have certain reservations about going to Baltimore.

In 1956, '57, and '58 we played exhibition games there before the opening of each season, and I knew they had problems. In those years we had to stay in Negro hotels, we couldn't go to the movies or the restaurants. I wondered if conditions had changed. I knew they must have changed some because Negro ballplayers were now staying downtown at the hotels with the rest of the ball club. But I wasn't sure about the rest of it, or how my family would be treated once we moved to Baltimore.

Right after the trade I read a statement from Baltimore that one of the reasons for the trade was because the Orioles wanted to interest Negro fans, bring them out to the ball park. This bothered me a bit. If having me in a Baltimore uniform would bring more Negroes to the ball park, all well and good. I didn't mind that. In Cincinnati, I knew a certain amount of Negro people would come out to the ball park to see me play. But I didn't want to be put in a position where I was going to have to make appearances before Negro groups, where I would be asked to make special pitches. I didn't want to be used by the ball club, I didn't want to be a tool. I was a little concerned about that but I can say now that the Baltimore ball club never did use me as a tool. They never even talked to me about going out and selling Baltimore baseball to the Negro population of the city.

And I was received real well in Baltimore from the time I arrived. My family was accepted well, too, although we did have a little trouble at the beginning finding a house. Once we moved in it worked out beautifully and that made it much easier on me to perform my job out on the field. I didn't have to worry about my family and I was able to concentrate fully on baseball.

But those were my main concerns after the trade was announced, those were the things I thought about. When I slept on it I felt much better. I felt I was very fortunate to be going to a good ball club. It could have been a lot worse. I could have been traded to Houston, or some ball club that usually finished around the bottom. But after going over in my mind the players I knew on the Orioles, I was relieved. Baltimore had been in the pennant race for the last couple of years and I knew this was a ball club with a good chance to win a pennant in 1966.

Now I looked on this change in my life as one more challenge. All my baseball life, I have looked at baseball as a series of challenges. Each ball game, each pitch, is a real challenge for me . . . a small challenge. But there have been the bigger ones—breaking into big-league baseball; the beaning in 1958 and having to overcome the fear of being hit again; having to bounce back and prove myself all over again after a bad year; the arrest in 1960 for carrying a gun, the feeling of letting down the kids of the country and the determination to make up for that. And now the new challenge, maybe the biggest one of all—making it in Baltimore. This one I looked forward to, this one I was eager to meet head-on.

15 *The Year of the Oriole*

It started for me in a hostile cracker town in the state of Georgia, my car indisposed back up the road, and this guy looking at me beady-eyed and saying, "What do you want, boy?" And I thought to myself, is this an omen, is this the kind of year it's going to be?

Everything was going along fine on my way to the Miami training camp of the Orioles, until I hit the interstate expressway in Georgia. I passed a car on the left and as I was easing back into the right lane, I saw an object lying in the road. I tried to miss it, but I didn't. It kicked up under the car hard and as I looked out of my rear-view window I saw what I thought was dust flying out from under the car. I said to myself, "Wow, that was a real hard blow."

It wasn't dust, it was smoke. I looked down at my gas gauge and it had gone from over a half-tank to almost empty and I said, "Oh, no, that put a hole in my gas tank."

Fortunately, I was near the exit on the expressway and I managed to get up the ramp and into a service station.

The attendant took one look and verified that there was a hole in my tank. He couldn't fix it and he told me there was no Cadillac dealer in town but to try a Pontiac dealer, who might be able to patch it up or replace the tank. I tried to make it to this town but I ran out of gas before I got there. I pulled over to the side of the road and went on foot the rest of the way, about a ten-minute walk.

I came into this Pontiac dealer's place. I must have stood around for an hour before anyone said anything to me. Then one of the men in the office finally looked up as if just noticing my presence. He said, "What do you want, boy?"

I explained to him what had happened and where my car was. He said, "Well, boy, we'll just have to wait until the wrecker comes back to tow you in."

I waited around for another hour and finally they went out and got my car. One of the Georgia gentlemen came out to look at it. He said, "Do you want us to fix it, boy, or do you want a new gas tank?"

I said, "Well, I'd like to get a new one if I can."

"We'll see what we can do."

He started to make some calls and while I waited someone came in, looked closely at me, and asked where I was going. I told him Miami, Florida.

"What do you do down there?" he asked.

"I'm a baseball player."

"What's your name?"

"Frank Robinson."

He looked at me and said, "Oh, Mr. Robinson, yes sir, we'll be glad to fix the gas tank as soon as we can." Things started to pick up a little then, after they found out who I was. I was *boy* no longer. Now I was *Mr.* Robinson.

They finally did find a gas tank for me and I ended up losing only three or four hours off my trip to Miami. It could have been worse, but the whole experience made me apprehensive. What I needed in 1966 was a tiger in my tank, not a hole, and this was a heckuva way to start things off.

I cruised into the state of Florida and reached this juncture with a sign pointing one way toward Miami and another sign pointing toward Tampa. And I had an overpowering urge to take the Tampa road and go visit my teammates. Up to now, the trade was still like a dream to me. I was coming in a stranger to most of the Oriole players and I already missed my old teammates. We were a close-knit group at Cincinnati and I was really tempted to take that road to

Tampa, see my buddies again, and spend a day or two with them.

But I thought better of it. I thought, I'm seven days late now. I better go on to Miami. Besides, if I ran into Mr. DeWitt, he might get confused and try to make another trade. So I went on.

The reason I was late reporting to camp was that I hadn't yet signed my contract. The ball club told the press that they had given me permission to clear up my affairs in Cincinnati. That was true, but I would have reported on time if I had signed. Nobody classified me as a holdout in 1966 but if you don't sign by the time spring training officially starts, that's what you are. That's what I was.

It was a minor problem, really. The Orioles had offered me the same contract that I received with Cincinnati in 1965. I didn't think it was a fair contract, although they were very nice about the whole thing. Harry Dalton, the Orioles' business manager, explained to me that it was his first year in signing major-league players, and that he would go over the figures again.

The Orioles' argument was that while I had a good year in Cincinnati in 1965, it hadn't been for Baltimore. They were saying, in effect, let's see what you can do for us. But I felt I should be rewarded for the good year that I had with Cincinnati. I didn't think it was right to sacrifice a raise because I was traded.

We went back and forth for a while. They upped the ante a bit but I still didn't think it was enough and by late February we hadn't come to an agreement. I was a little concerned because I did want to get off on the right foot with the ball club. But I felt I owed it to myself and my family to get as much as I thought I deserved for the coming year.

Mr. Dalton finally persuaded me to come to Miami. I hadn't wanted to come without signing because it meant I would have to pay my own expenses. But we weren't that far apart at the time, thirty-five hundred dollars, so I agreed to go to Miami.

I got into the hotel about 10 P.M. on the night of March 7. The next morning I went right out to the park. Harry Dalton and I sat down in his office and in ten or fifteen minutes, with give and take on both sides, we got the salary straightened out and I put my name on the dotted line.

I felt much better now and took my equipment into the clubhouse and met Hank Bauer for the first time.

He welcomed me warmly and told me he was real happy to have me on the ball club. The first thing he asked me was about my arm.

That impressed me, that he was aware of my arm problem. I always have trouble with the arm during spring training. The arm has bothered me every spring since 1954, when I first injured it. It usually takes me about two or three weeks to work it out. Hank told me to take it easy on the arm and let him know when I was ready to play.

That first morning I took calisthenics, threw a little bit on the sidelines, and then got into the batting cage.

My new teammates were on me pretty good, right from the start. One of them said, "Will you look at that guy in there? There is a real Frank Robinson after all. He's not a myth."

I started off hitting popups and Luis Aparicio, who was out by second base, shouted, "Ah, I thought we got a home-run hitter and instead we got a guy that pops up. Bring back Pappas."

There was an intrasquad game that day and I didn't start. But about halfway through, Bauer came over and asked me if I wanted to pinch-hit. I said, sure. I got up against Dick Hall and lined a double down the left-field line.

I got into three exhibition games as a pinch-hitter and did nothing each time. Finally, I was put in the starting lineup in a game against Washington. In the first inning I went up against Buster Narum. I hit the ball over the left-field fence.

As I rounded the bases, I didn't hear a whisper coming from the Orioles' bench. What's going on? I crossed home plate and Brooks Robinson, on-deck, turned his back on me. In the dugout nobody looked at me, nobody shook my hand, nobody said anything. Silence . . . Finally, I barked, "Well, you know what you all can do." That broke it. They all started laughing and came up and congratulated me. The silent period was over. I was a member of the team.

That was a very pleasant spring training period. I was hitting better than I usually hit in the spring. That was because of a change in my stance.

In the spring of 1965 I started to hold my bat straight up instead of laying it back on my shoulder as I had always done in the past. And I didn't bend at the waist quite as much as I had. The change worked. I hit .360 the month of April, which is about 180 points more than my usual April average. The whole year wasn't that strong, unfortunately. I wasn't consistent. I struck out one hundred times for the first time in my career, but I think that was because of the change I made. I wasn't able to handle a number of pitches that I had before.

In the spring of '66, I was tempted to change back. As a matter of fact, I did hit a little bit my old way, but then I went back to the new way—the bat held straight up—and stuck with it. And I was glad I did.

The only things that marred that first spring with the Orioles were more comments from Bill DeWitt.

Two or three weeks into spring training a reporter for one of the Miami papers came into our clubhouse and asked me, "Why do you think the Reds traded you?"

I said, "I really don't know. I'd like to know myself."

He said, "Maybe I'll ask DeWitt."

I said, "That's a good idea. Why don't you ask him?"

The reporter phoned Bill DeWitt and Mr. DeWitt's answer was that I was an *old* thirty. First he said, "We traded him to strengthen the ball club because we need pitching." Then he stuck in the needle. He said that if I had been twenty-six he probably wouldn't have traded me. He also cited my medical record, but he never did explain what he meant by that.

When I read the interview I was very upset. If he had stuck to the one fact—that he had traded me to strengthen his ball club—I would have had no complaints. But I couldn't understand why he would say I was an old thirty. It seemed that I had aged badly between the end of the 1965 season and December 9.

He never did explain what he meant about my medical record, either. In the five years that he and I were together on the club, I played in 153 games, 162 games, 140 games, 156 games, 156 games. I never missed a game because of sickness and many times I played with injuries. The only times I didn't play were when I was hurt and not going well, anyway.

As the season went on, Mr. DeWitt kept up the barrage: "He never had a year like that for us . . ." "Wait until July, August . . ." "Wait and see how he comes out at the end of the year . . ." "In the ten years he played for us we won only one pennant." I guess he was just frustrated because I was doing so well and the fellows he had traded me for weren't doing so well. But some of his statements, I felt, were way out of line.

For instance he accused me of a grave crime; that I spent all my time shining my shoes. What he meant was that I was shining my shoes in the clubhouse when he thought I should be out on the field taking hitting practice. Well, I don't always take hitting practice. I didn't with Cincinnati, and I don't with Baltimore. I think that if you're going well you don't need all that batting practice. I think you can get into bad habits. You get in there and you start moving your head and swinging too hard and things like that. And in the summer months especially, I cut down on batting practice to save myself for the game. But if the manager ever told me to go out and hit, I would.

Mr. Hoffberger, the owner of the Orioles, was always on me in 1966 about my shoe-shining exercises. He came into the clubhouse one day and said, "Look at that Robinson, he's always shining his shoes."

I tossed him a coin. "Here's a quarter," I said. "Have your shoes shined." He kept the quarter, too.

If I had done that with Mr. DeWitt, I would have been run out of the clubhouse. But that was the difference between the Baltimore front office and Cincinnati. There is a good, loose atmosphere, a close feeling between the Baltimore front office and their players. There was never that feeling in Cincinnati when Mr. DeWitt ran the team.

That good, relaxed atmosphere began to grow on me as the exhibition season wore on and I began to feel that we had a real good shot at the American League pennant. But there were problems. We had Paul Blair in center field, trying to make it as a regular for the first time. We had Andy Etchebarren behind the plate. He hadn't put in a full season in the majors and he came into camp as no. 3 catcher. But he was going to be the first-string catcher because we lost our no. 1 man, Dick Brown, who underwent a brain operation. We had Davey Johnson, a kid, taking over second base. So you began to wonder. You're going to have a kid behind the plate. You're going to have a kid in center field, and a kid on second base. Also Boog Powell was coming off a bad year and we didn't know how far he was going to come back. Luis Aparicio was also coming off a bad year and we didn't know how far he could come, either. And we had a young pitching staff. There were just a lot of question marks.

But there was no question mark at third base. Before coming to Baltimore I had always felt that Ken Boyer and Jim Davenport were the best third basemen in baseball. I couldn't believe that Brooks Robinson could be any better. But after watching him that spring I found that he was far better than I had heard he was. He was the best I'd ever seen at that position. When the ball was hit down the third-base side of the field, I found myself in the outfield just standing there, watching him, like a fan. The plays he was making at third base amazed me.

Brooks and I got along very well, as well as any two ballplayers can get along. He is a friendly person and an easy person to get to know and he was very helpful to me from the time I got to spring training. He helped make it a lot easier for me to adjust to playing with Baltimore.

In the lineup Hank Bauer had worked out, I was going to bat third, and Brooks fourth. This was a switch for me because I had been the no. 4 hitter in most of my years with Cincinnati. I had to adjust my thinking a bit. The no. 4 hitter can't be as choosy about the pitch he swings at. For instance, he usually goes after the 3-and-1 pitch. The no. 3 batter can take it more often, take the base on balls rather than try to drive in the run. Batting third is a guarantee that you're going to hit in the first inning, and the job of the first three hitters is to try and get on base. My thinking was that I had to change a little, take a few walks, go for the single to move the runner into scoring position, and not worry about the big base hit, sacrifice myself a little bit and work the pitchers a little bit more. As I accustomed myself to the position, I found it more fun because I had more options at my command.

By the time we headed north, I was really looking forward to the opening of the season. For ten seasons I had opened at home, a tradition because Cincinnati is the oldest major-league team. Now, for the first time in my big-league career, I would open on the road. I liked that because it would give me a chance to get my feet on the ground. I think I might have been a little less relaxed had we opened in Baltimore. There might have been a bit more pressure on me.

The fact that we were opening in Boston didn't hurt,

either. Fenway Park has that inviting left-field wall, 315 feet down the line, and I figured they would be trying to pitch me inside, at least in the first series. If I could get around on the ball with the fence out there, I figured to get a big base hit.

Top of the first inning, on Opening Day, April 12, I went in against Earl Wilson. His first pitch was an inside fast ball and it caught me on the forearm. As I jogged to first base for the 119th time in the major leagues because of a direct hit on my anatomy, I thought: Here we go again.

The arm felt fine just as soon as Brooks stepped in and hit a home run over that left-field wall.

The whole day felt fine, in fact. Between the Robinsons, there were five hits, three runs, two home runs, four runs batted in, and a stolen base. My second time up, I singled, my third time up I hit my first American League home run.

We won that game, and the next two against the Red Sox, and I hit a home run in each game. One came on a 3-and-0 pitch when manager Bauer flashed me the "hit" sign. It was a pleasure and I hit one off Dave Morehead that went over the left-field wall.

Hank gave me the hit sign on 3-and-0 several times through the season, but they didn't always work. Once late in the year we were playing in Chicago. I wasn't going too well but Hank flashed me the hit sign on 3-and-0. I couldn't believe it. I was reluctant to swing at the pitch even if it was going to be a strike. But I thought, well, if it's a good strike and I can handle the pitch, I'll swing at it, because if I don't and it's a strike, the manager will say to me, "You know you had to hit, didn't you?"

That's what Hank always said. So I thought I better swing. It turned out not to be the type of pitch that I could really handle. The ball was inside on me a little bit and I popped it up to the third baseman.

I went back and told the manager I was surprised. "You had no business giving me the hit sign the way I'm going."

"I wouldn't have," Hank said scornfully, "if I knew you were going to take a swing like that."

Hank is a great needler. In fact the whole team was made up of needlers, and that's what kept us loose all year long. Among other things, they were always on me about my legs. I have thin legs and Boog Powell, who is a good-natured guy, started calling me "Pencils."

We'd get on a bus and he'd holler, "Pencils, if you didn't have feet, your legs would stick in the ground." Boog is a real big one, about 240, so I just happened to come up with a nickname for him—Crisco. "What's that mean?" a puzzled writer asked me one day. I said, "Shortening, you know, that's what it comes from." What I was telling Boog was that he was fat.

On top of the nicknames there were the practical jokes— the hotfoots, sneezing powder, disappearing ink, rubber snakes. We'd sneak up behind Luis Aparicio, who really reacted to these things, place a towel around his neck, and holler, "Snake!" It got so in the periods when hotfoots were the rage that before you went into the clubhouse you took off your shoes and put them in your locker. And when you got ready to leave, you walked to the door of the clubhouse and then you put your shoes back on. Because if you had them on and you turned your back for one second, they'd stick a couple of matches in your shoe and light you up.

The joking never stopped. I remember one midsummer trip we had to take a chartered plane because the regular airlines were on strike. Well, that created all sorts of possibilities, especially since the chartered line was normally a freight carrier. Taxiing down the runway the plane was slowed to a halt because of a problem with one of the engines. We were in the midst of our favorite card game, Buck-Up, when I tossed five dollars into the pot, put on my suit coat, and said, "Open the door."

On the return trip, from Boston, we traveled with the same

airline and I dressed in a black undertaker's suit. "I'm ready in case we crash," I reassured my teammates.

All that clowning and joking served a purpose, I think. The mood of a ball club is very important. If you have happy players, they're going to put out extra and do things that a discontented ballplayer won't do. And we had that good mood, that good attitude. We were a young club and had the type of fellows who liked to laugh and joke a lot. These kids were subject to a lot of pressure, and the horsing around relaxed them a bit. If an individual was going through a period when he wasn't hitting or pitching well, the jokes and things served the purpose of cutting the tension a bit. But when it came time for the ball game, that was it. Then it was time to get serious, and everyone did.

It was a pleasure playing for Hank Bauer. He was built up to be the real tough ex-Marine, a guy who's supposed to growl and everybody jumps. But he doesn't growl much. He's one ex-ballplayer who, when he became manager, didn't forget what it was to be a player. He always looked out for our welfare. These was a very good relationship between Bauer and his coaches and the players. It was like a family. You could discuss your problems with Hank and he was very tolerant about your mistakes. He wouldn't get too mad when you made a mistake because he knew you were a professional and no matter how young you were, you wouldn't be likely to make that mistake again.

Hank wasn't a big strategist. He just didn't believe in too much strategy. There were very few take signs, very little hit-and-run situations in the 1966 season. His idea was to put his best eight men out there, plus the pitcher, and let them do the job, let them do what they could do best.

After we went around the league the first time that spring of 1966 and had met to go over the players on the other clubs, we only had two meetings the rest of the year. Both came late in the season when we were struggling through a bad period. Hank just reminded us that we were a good ball club and to go out and play good, sound baseball. We had a big lead at the time but we could easily get into a rut, a losing attitude. And the meetings helped us. At least we sat down and talking things over aired things out a bit.

We established our lead in the American League early in the season. We were in and out of first place in April and May and settled there around the fifteenth of June. Our first crucial series came in May when we met the Indians, who were then running neck-and-neck with us. On May 8, we played the Indians a doubleheader before forty-nine thousand home fans and that turned out to be one of the biggest days of my life.

We won the first game, 8–3, but Luis Tiant was the Indians' starting pitcher in the second game and he had pitched three straight shutouts in his first three starts. Everybody expected this to be a real tight ball game.

In the bottom of the first we got a man on and Tiant's first pitch to me was a fast ball down and in. I hit it real good. I knew it was a home run as soon as I hit it, but when I got back to the dugout the fellows floored me. They said the ball had gone clear out of the stadium (451 feet on the fly, 540 feet on the roll, the tape-measure engineers said later).

I said, "No, you're joking, you're pulling my leg."

When I went out to right field at the end of the inning, the public address announcer hushed the crowd. "Frank Robinson's home run," he intoned, "was the first fair ball ever hit completely out of Memorial Stadium."

The fans started applauding and it built up and up and up, into a big roar, and then everyone was on their feet giving me a standing ovation. It seemed like they were standing for five hours. I was touched, really touched. I couldn't believe this was happening to me. I thought it was wonderful for the fans to show me such respect for what I considered just another home run. It made me more relaxed, too. Up to then I felt the Baltimore fans were holding off their approval of me, saying, we'll just wait and see if he's really good, if he's really got it. It made me feel very happy to be accepted that way. I felt I was at home.

I went five-and-seven that day and raised my average over .400 and took the lead in the American League batting race.

But the average didn't stay up there. Toward the end of May I slipped almost one hundred points. Later, I went back up to .349, then slipped back to about .300 before I leveled off for the rest of the season. One time I went into a slump, it was my teammate, Davey Johnson, who spotted the flaw and got me out of it.

Davey, who was only twenty-three and a rookie in 1966, had been watching me from spring training and we talked to each other a lot about hitting. We both put our back foot in the same place in the batter's box. Davey hit behind me in the lineup and, when he came up, my mark was usually still there. But during this slump—I was three-for-eighteen—he noticed my back foot wasn't where it should be. I had moved up about six inches in the batter's box and I wasn't really getting around on the ball.

Davey was a little reluctant to come and say anything to me about it. He told a writer later, "I'd never tell *him* what to do." And it went on like that for a week and I knew I wasn't getting around on the ball like I should. But I couldn't figure out why. I went through my checklist. Was I keeping my head still? Was I watching the ball? Was I going into the ball? Was I getting the bat out front? Was I holding the bat too low or too high? Was I standing the way that I always do? Was I in the right place in the batter's box? I thought I was but Davey finally told me I wasn't. I moved back those six inches and it made the difference. I saw the ball better. I didn't rush my swing. I was more relaxed. I went on a twelve-for-seventeen binge and raised my average from .308 to .328.

The kind of advice that Davey gave me, where he can raise a fellow's average so dramatically, is rare in baseball. When you're in a slump, you usually can't point to one thing and say, this is it. Each slump is different. Sometimes you may be a little tired and fall into bad habits. Or you may get overanxious and start swinging from the heels, trying to hit every ball out of the park. Or you start to pull outside pitches too much and end up pulling everything that's thrown up there. Other times, too, you aren't watching the ball; you lose track of it and have to pick it up again. Or you might start lunging at off-speed pitches. Very seldom is there one thing you can point to and say, this is what's causing my slump.

One thing I don't particularly care for is receiving tips from players. The more information I get, a lot of times the worse off I am. Each ballplayer, I think, has his own ideas about a pitcher—a pitcher's fast ball, a pitcher's curve, how good it is and how much it breaks. But I'm the type who has to find out for himself. And I found out early in the 1966 season that when I was told about a pitcher—that he had a good fast ball or curve ball—I went up there looking for too much, expecting too much, and I was anxious and didn't hit well. So I decided to just go up there and look for what I could see, and I was better off that way. As the year went on in Baltimore, I told the fellows, don't tell me how good his fast ball is or his curve ball. All I want to know is if he has a trick—a knuckle ball or a slow curve, or if he drops down and throws to the side, things like that.

The duel between pitcher and batter is a cat-and-mouse affair, after all, and never more so for me than in 1966. I didn't know the American League pitchers and they didn't know me, but if anyone had the edge it was them; they had the ball, they knew what they were going to try.

On defense, there were adjustments to be made, too. I had to learn how each player should be played, and I had to get used to different ball parks. Probably the one that took the most getting used to was Yankee Stadium in New York. The right-field area at Yankee Stadium is unlike that of any stadium in the National League, except perhaps for Pittsburgh. The foul line is very close to the stands and there's not too much running room in that corner and you have to play the outfield a little cagier than you would in another park. Still, my most enjoyable moment in the outfield in 1966 came out there against the Yankees.

We were playing a twi-night doubleheader on June 21. We were leading in the first game, 7–5, in the bottom of the ninth. The Yankees had two men on and two out and Roy White was at the plate.

Stu Miller was pitching for us. Stu's nickname is "Bullet." That's because he throws the slowest fast ball and the slowest set of curves in all of baseball. With Miller throwing to White, I was leaning toward the line, figuring on White to pull the ball just a little more than he normally would. I was guarding against a line drive being hit down the line and maybe going into the stands for a home run. A home run at this point beats us, and we had come too far in this ball game to lose on a 296-foot dink shot. If White hit the ball to right-center, that would be all right. I felt I could get to it a little quicker because I move better going to my right than I do to my left.

Well, White caught hold of one and pulled it, but not as much as I thought he would. It was hit to my right, a line drive, and it was up pretty good.

This was about eight in the evening, that twilight zone between day and night, and it was difficult to follow the ball. I saw it when it left the bat, but then I lost it momentarily.

But I kept running to the right.

I had been playing on the grass and I ran back and over, about twenty to twenty-five feet, at an angle. I hit the warning track and just as I got to the fence, which is only four feet high, I had to jump and turn at the same time to catch the ball. I was up in the air facing the infield when I caught the ball and hit the fence.

The jolt carried me into the stands. I landed in a little space between the fence and the first row of seats. I was holding my glove up while my legs were dangling on the fence. The idea was to try to get myself off the fence and back up on the field. So I dropped my feet over into the stands and then I pushed myself up with my gloved hand, the ball still in it. At no time was the ball out of my glove. I never juggled the ball, the ball never moved, or rolled.

I got up slowly, as best I could with people tugging at me, trying to get the ball. I had to fight them off and climb back on the field at the same time. Paul Blair came over from center field and helped me.

The umpire was right out there and he extended his hand, the out sign, and I just trotted off the field into the clubhouse. We had won, 7–5. The game was over. But it was not over for Yankee manager Ralph Houk.

He created quite a storm out there. I didn't mind that. It's his job to argue for his team. But I didn't like him questioning my honesty. He said he knew that I didn't catch the ball. Furthermore, he said he knew that I knew I didn't catch the ball. Ralph, I caught the ball. There was no way I could have recovered the ball and stuck it in my glove *after* I fell in, not with the fans all around me. They would have picked up the ball and been gone before I could have moved.

Houk seemed to take pleasure all year in putting me down. In one newspaper article, the writer was taking a poll on who would be the American League's Most Valuable Player— Brooks or me—and Houk went out of his way to knock me again. He said that I was just an ordinary outfielder and they could always put somebody out there to replace me, that I couldn't go toward the line and catch balls that other outfielders could catch. That kind of bugged me. I don't think I'm thin-skinned when it comes to criticism, but I guess I am when I think it's unfair or unjust. And I felt his criticism of my ability and his questioning of my honesty was unjust and uncalled for.

Houk really stirred the natives that night. The second game was something. Once I went for a ball hit by Elston

Howard and was just about to catch it at the fence when a fan grabbed my arm and tried to pull it away from the ball. I caught it okay, but I wonder what would have happened if the ball had dropped.

Later in the game the people out there began to chant, "There's no way you're getting in here again, Robinson." And I knew they meant it. They were throwing all kinds of debris at me. They threw garbage, they threw boxes, they even threw cherry bombs. And I was booed whenever I showed my face, even in the on-deck circle. It was amusing to me in a way because usually when a ballplayer makes an outstanding play he's applauded for it. And I believe that was the best catch of my entire career.

Hank told me after that game that he had received a report from a policeman that some people were "out to get Frank Robinson." I told Hank, "You'd better not run a bed check tonight, because neither you nor anybody else is getting in."

We lost that second game to the Yankees, but no booing, no garbage throwing—nothing was going to stop the Orioles in 1966.

16 Triple Crown

We went into the All-Star break leading the league by eight games. I was fortunate to be selected for the All-Star team. It's quite an honor to have played on the All-Star team for both leagues. But the game itself was a bust. The National League beat us 2–1 and it was the other Robinson who made all the noise. While I went 0-for-4, Brooks had three hits and made some great fielding plays and, deservedly, was named the game's MVP. My only contribution was a pregame piece of advice to our starting pitcher, Denny McLain.

Willie Mays was to be the first batter for the National League and I told Denny that Willie likes to hit the first pitch, especially if it's a fast ball. I told Denny to throw Mays anything but the fast ball on the first pitch because I knew Willie would be looking for it. So he threw Willie a breaking ball and he went real bad on it and he eventually struck out.

Then, four days later, we faced Denny McLain in a key game. Right after the All-Star break we went into Detroit for a three-game series. We lost the first two games and that cut our lead back to six games. McLain was having a fine year up to the time—he had won thirteen games—but we hopped right on him for six runs in the first two innings and beat Detroit, 8–2. We went into Chicago and won two out of three and then Detroit came into Baltimore. We won all three games and were back in business again.

But the Tigers had been tough for us early in the year. In fact, in one game against Detroit I almost got thrown out of the game, and that had only happened to me three times in the majors.

Despite my aggressive nature, I have been very careful about annoying umpires, not wanting to hurt my team by getting thrown out of a game over an argument that I couldn't win anyway.

The first time I was thrown out was over a difference of opinion about a pitch. The umpire, Shag Crawford, called a strike which I regarded as questionable. I didn't say too much about it then but when, on the next pitch, he called another questionable strike, I turned around and looked at him.

"What are you looking at?" he said.

I said, "Nothing when I look at you."

I quickly left that game.

My next run-in came a few years later when we felt the plate umpire, Dusty Boggess, was calling a bad game against us. The bench got on him pretty heavy and he was a little angry and threatened to throw a few of the players off the bench. When I came up to bat I said, "Take it easy, c'mon, it's not that bad."

He said, "Go on, get in the batter's box."

I said, "I'll get in there when I want to."

So then he told the pitcher to throw the ball. I was standing just outside the batter's box and the pitcher threw the ball and when the umpire tells the pitcher to pitch in that situation it's an automatic strike, no matter where the pitch goes.

I stepped into the batter's box and just before the pitcher made the next pitch, I stepped out. Boggess said, "Get back in there!"

I said, "I can get out when I want to."

"You didn't ask for my permission," he said. "Get back in there."

"I don't have to ask for your permission."

Boggess told the pitcher to pitch again. Strike two. Two strikes when I wasn't even in the batter's box. A little argument broke out then, and I was thrown out of the game.

The third time I was thrown out it cost me money.

It was on another questionable call at the plate, and I was arguing with the umpire, trying to explain my side of it. Shag Crawford came in from his infield position to break up the argument. And I tried to tell Shag what had happened. All he said was, "Okay, let's go, let's start the game again."

I said, "I'll get back in the batter's box when I'm ready," and then he threw me out.

Then they claimed I said what no National League ballplayer is supposed to say, a taboo word which, when uttered, means a five-hundred-dollar fine and an automatic three-day suspension. Dick Sisler, our manager, and Tom Haller, the Giants' catcher, were both at home plate at the time and neither one heard me say the word. I did say something else, which entitled me to being thrown out of the game, but not a suspension.

There must have been at least some doubt in the umpires' minds because the president of the National League only gave me a two-day suspension and a $150 fine.

But all in all I have tried to limit my run-ins with umpires. In all my career, I have argued only on plays that I felt were *very* important, and where I felt I was completely in the right.

Such a time was in this game at home against Detroit. There were two outs in the ninth inning and we were down by a 3–2 score. I doubled and third-base coach Billy Hunter hustled out to talk to me.

At this time I was playing with a deep pull in the back of my thigh. I was bandaged from the top of the thigh to mid-calf, and Hunter wanted to know if I thought I could run all right. I knew I couldn't run as well as I normally could, but I told Billy I thought I could score from second base on a good hit. I left the decision up to him if he wanted to put in a runner, but I really wanted to stay in the game. If we tied the game, I wanted to be around when it went into extra innings.

So he let me stay in and the next hitter, Brooks, stroked a

hot line drive into short left field. When the ball was hit I was on the go, but I could tell that I was going to have to move to make it.

Willie Horton, the Tigers' left fielder, picked up the ball cleanly and made a good throw. I was barreling toward home debating with myself which way to go in. Bill Freehan, the catcher, was up in front of the plate, straddling the line. I said to myself, either I can go straight in and even if he doesn't have the ball right away he can probably block me off; or, I can go around him. I decided to go around him and I decided to go in head first.

Going in head first had two advantages. First, it was the quickest way. You naturally have to slow down a little bit to slide in feet first. And the way he was straddling the line and blocking the plate I would have had to go around him and then come back and tag the plate. Secondly, he would have less of a target to shoot at. I could get around him easier going head first and be able to tag the plate at the same time. This way I was just giving him a hand to tag.

I slid head-first, threw my body out, and tagged the plate with my hand as I went by him.

I never felt Freehan tag me, but the umpire called me out. "No! No! No!" I cried. "He didn't touch me!"

The umpire said, "Yes he did. He got you on the shoulder."

I said, "If he hit me on the shoulder he'd have turned me around from the force of it." But it was no good and we lost the ball game on that play.

Later in the clubhouse a reporter asked Freehan if he had tagged me. I have never yet heard a player deny that he tagged a guy out. Freehan said, yes, he tagged me on the right hand as I went by. So there were two different stories, right there. The umpire said he'd got me on the shoulder; the catcher said he got me on the hand. A few days later they published a sequence of photos on the play. They showed that the whole top half of my body was on the plate, by him, before he had even moved to tag me.

That was okay, though. Most of the breaks went our way in 1966. After we beat Detroit those three games at home in July our next big series came against Minnesota. And we swept five games from them. That pushed Detroit way back and wrecked Minnesota's hopes, because they were starting to play good ball at the time.

It's lucky we did run up that big lead—I think it reached 13½ games at one time—because we started to go bad in August. By that, I mean we only played .500 ball the rest of the way. But there were reasons.

For one, Brooks had had a tremendous first half, I don't think any player could have had a better half-season than he had. But he tailed off in the second half. Boog Powell had his troubles early but came on late in May and almost tore the league apart by himself. Then late in the season he came up with a chip on his finger which slowed him a bit.

Manager Hank Bauer had said before the season that the team with the fewest injuries would win the pennant. He was wrong. We just about led the league in that department, and won anyhow. Davey Johnson broke his toe and later took fourteen stitches in the other leg. Curt Blefary broke out in hives. Andy Etchebarren was hurt for a while. Steve Barber and Wally Bunker came up with sore arms. In fact, almost everyone on the staff, except for Dave McNally and Moe Drabowsky, had sore arms at one time or other.

I hurt my right knee in a June game against the Yankees. It was the seventh or eighth inning and I singled to right field. I was going to first base at a normal rate of speed, and as I rounded the base and stopped to go back, I felt something pop in my knee. It didn't hurt right off. I took my lead at first and after the pitch, as I started back to first base, the knee pained me again.

I called time and put my weight on it. It felt kind of weak so I left the game. I still didn't think it was anything; I felt it was the type of injury that would clear up overnight. But the knee still bothered me the next day and was swollen

pretty bad. I wrapped it each day after that and played that
way for the rest of the season. There were times it bothered
me and times it didn't, but it never healed—it kept filling
up with fluid and the ligaments stretched—so I finally did
have it operated on after the season.

That was my only injury in '66 save for a pull in the back
of my leg, which lasted a couple of weeks and slowed me up a
bit. I figure I got off pretty easy. One of my other nicknames,
you know, is "Tape." That's from the fact that I always have
tape on me somewhere or other during the season. I'm always bruised or broken up, with jammed thumbs, sprained
ankles, strawberries on my rear from sliding—things like that.
When my teammates can't see any tape on me, they get concerned. They ask me worriedly, "Got any on?" And I say,
"Yep, you better believe I have some on someplace."
That makes them feel better. Once one of the guys ticked
off my various injuries, and another one said:

"From the waist up, you're OK?"

I said, "Sure, if I dangle my hands below my waist."

My teammates get on me about the tape and also about
a so-called eccentricity, wearing three pairs of socks. Some
writers have concluded I do that to make my legs look
heavier. Well, three pairs of socks aren't going to make *my*
legs look any larger. Actually, I wear a sanitary—the long
white socks—then I put on a short thin sweat sock underneath, which comes about halfway up my leg, and then another sanitary on top of that. The reason for this is to cushion
the bottom of my feet from the spikes underneath. It gets
to be a grind with these spikes on the hard field day after
day, and the socks keep the calluses off the bottom of my
feet. Also, I have a tendency to kick myself on my ankles
when I'm running, and the three socks offer me some protection there, too.

It's all part of what I call the constant fight for survival,
for your livelihood in baseball. You must simply do everything within your power to protect your livelihood and you

must never give in, especially when you think you're right.

The only unpleasant situation for me in the 1966 season with the Orioles came when I felt my livelihood was being compromised.

We were playing the White Sox at home. There was a man on third, one out, and I hit a chopper down the third-base line. It wasn't hit very well and Gene Freese, the White Sox third baseman, was playing me deep, in back of the bag. He came in and fielded the ball on the dead run. But he threw the ball home into the dirt and the run scored. Naturally, I was safe on first.

The scorer, a Baltimore sportswriter, gave Freese an error on that play, which took away the run batted in for me. I figured the worst it should have been called was a fielder's choice, because Freese could have probably thrown me out at first, and it was a tough play. But I kept my thoughts to myself.

About three weeks later, the same situation arose. One of our players hit the ball down the third-base line, the pitcher came over, threw home, the catcher couldn't hold the ball, and the runner scored. This time the same official scorer gave the batter a hit, and an RBI.

After the game I cornered the scorer in the locker room. I was doing a slow burn. I asked him how he could have scored that one way and mine another. He told me he didn't remember the other play, the one where I lost the RBI. That's when I really got mad. I hollered at him and ate him out, and it was the wrong thing to do. I was flat out of line doing it the way I did. What I should have done was get him alone and try to calmly discuss the thing. But I was so doggone mad.

A lot of times when you argue with a scorer—and I think all the ballplayers have such arguments at one time or another—he'll say, "That's only one, what are you worried about one base hit?" Well, it isn't one base hit. It's one hit here and one there and pretty soon it means the difference

between five and ten points on your average. It's your livelihood you're arguing about.

I don't think official scorers are consistent enough in their
calls. They're only human and some of them do lean a little
bit toward certain players. A situation came up in 1966
when we were facing the Yankees and Bobby Richardson
had to leave the game. Horace Clarke moved into second
base and Curt Blefary hit a ball to the right of Clarke. Clarke
was on the dead run and took the ball backhanded, but it
went off his glove. They called it an error. They said if Bobby
Richardson had been playing he would have made the play.
That's a heckuva way to make a decision, to compare one guy
with another.

There was another case when one of our players popped the
ball down the first-base line. Whitey Ford, the pitcher, came
over toward first base, started to pick up the ball right on
the line, almost with his back toward first, and didn't come
up with the ball. It was called an error. They said Whitey
Ford should have made the play. If it were any other pitcher,
a pitcher without a reputation as a good fielder, it would
have been called a hit.

Well, what can be done about the situation? I would like
to see *three* official scorers for each game, not one. Two
could be from the home side, one from the visiting team.
There would be an official scorer-in-chief, who would do the
actual scoring. But when a questionable play came up, he
would check with the other two scorers and take a vote. The
majority would rule. I don't know if this would solve all the
sins of official scoring, but I think it would help and I'd like to
see it tried.

Other than that, I can't think of a single unpleasant incident that happened to me during the 1966 season. Unless
of course you want to count the day I almost drowned.

We were enjoying an off-day outing at a fan's house. This
fellow had a beautiful big swimming pool and a lot of the

players and their wives were taking advantage of the pool. I was wearing a sports shirt and a pair of slacks, sitting in a lounging chair by poolside, talking with some of the other players who weren't swimming. Then the horseplay started. Curt Blefary was threatening to throw everybody in the pool who wasn't in already, clothed or not. A couple of the guys came up and grabbed me and said, "Okay, you're going in."

I said, "No, I don't swim."

"That doesn't matter. You're going in, anyway."

"Wait a minute," I said, "let me take my clothes off." And they very reluctantly let me go.

So I went in and put on a pair of swimming trunks. I figured I'd jump in the shallow end, get wet, stay around for a while, and then they'd probably leave me alone. I was going to outsmart them.

I jumped in at the shallow end all right, but what I didn't realize at the time was that when I came up, I was more than halfway down the pool, more toward the deep end than the shallow end.

I couldn't get a grip on anything. I went down once, came up, and hollered for help. There were people all around, just standing and talking, but it was pretty noisy at the time, and they didn't hear me.

I went down for a second time and then came up and was really panicky. I hollered, "Help, help, help!" I held my arms straight up in the air thinking someone would see me. And I started down for the third time.

Now I was tired and couldn't get back up again. I thought, this is it. I can just see the headlines—"Frank Robinson Drowned at Players' Party." That was the one thought that went through my mind. Then, all of a sudden, I felt a hand reach for me and I said, oh boy, they got me.

Somebody was trying to push me, but he lost contact. And I thought, oh no, here we go again.

Then I felt the contact again and I was being pushed over

to the side of the pool. And a couple of guys lifted me up out of the water.

I lay there panting, but I was all right. I hadn't taken any water in my lungs and I felt fine. It was Andy Etchebarren who saved my life. He said the reason he lost contact with me the first time was that he thought I might be kidding, so he hadn't taken a real deep breath of air. He had to go back up and get another deep breath and then come down and get me.

Everyone was surprised. They all thought I was kidding. They thought I could swim. Even my wife, who *knows* I can't swim, thought I was kidding. But I wasn't and I was very lucky to get out of that little mess.

So, you see, we had our little problems in 1966, our little misfortunes. But none of them were going to stop us. No matter what happened, we were going to win it.

On August 31, 1966, which happened to be my thirty-first birthday, we played an important game with the Indians. We had lost four in a row and were trying to fight out of it and Sam McDowell was pitching against us. All year long McDowell had given us a rough time. We were beating him regularly, but they were all low-scoring games. McDowell doesn't have just a great fast ball, he has excellent off-speed pitches, too—his breaking ball, his slider, his change-up. He got a lot of strikeouts with those pitches and that really impressed me.

He had us 1–0 going into the eighth inning. Up to then he had allowed only four hits and we were really staring down the mouth of the cannon, a fifth straight loss nudging at us hard. But with two outs in the eighth, McDowell hit Curt Blefary. And, suddenly, he left the ball game, complaining of a sore arm. So they brought in Luis Tiant.

Tiant's first pitch to me was a fast ball up and away and I hit it over the right-center-field fence and that put us ahead 2–1. We got three more runs in the ninth and won 5–1, and it was the best birthday present I received all day.

That really took us out of a tailspin because we lost our next two games. It would have been seven losses in a row if we hadn't won that game in Cleveland. It might have been a different pennant race. That one ball game was the difference.

By this time I had pulled well ahead for the home run lead in the American League, and when Boog Powell got hurt, I took the lead in runs batted in. And the talk began about my chances for winning the Triple Crown, something that hadn't been accomplished in baseball since Mickey Mantle did it in 1956.

The big question mark seemed to be the batting title. Tony Oliva had won the title two years in a row and was certainly capable of winning it again. I felt he would be my major competitor. He's an amazing youngster. He hits for average, he hits the long ball consistently, he hits to left field, right field, and center field, he moves the ball around real well and runs good and doesn't strike out much. He's going to be an outstanding ballplayer for many, many years.

I didn't know whether I could beat him out. In the last couple of months of the season he would be on top, then I would be on top, and it went back and forth like that until the last week of the season. I thought I had a chance at the batting crown but I was battling an outstanding player.

We faced Minnesota the last ball games of the season and Oliva still had an outside chance to catch me. The pennant race was over now but there seemed to be more pressure on my teammates than ever before. Especially the pitchers. They felt they had to get Oliva out to insure my winning the Triple Crown. I didn't want them to feel that way. One even came over and said, "I was thinking of walking him."

"That's wrong," I said, "I don't want you to do that."

Honestly, there was more pressure on them than on me about the Triple Crown thing. One writer asked me if I would sit out the Minnesota series. I said no. I intended to go out and do the best I could, like I always do.

Oliva and I posed for pictures before one of those games and I wished him good luck and he wished me good luck, and then I went out in the first game against Minnesota and got two hits. One was a line drive I hit off my fists down the left-field line. The other was a high hopper. Rich Rollins, the third baseman, had to wait for it and couldn't come up with it. And that did it. I ended at .316, Oliva at .307. My forty-nine home runs and 122 runs batted in gave me the other two legs on the Triple Crown and, for good measure, I led the league in runs scored with 122.

That was thrill enough, becoming a Triple Crown winner. But my biggest thrill came earlier, when we went to Kansas City on September 20.

The pressure was still on then. We were still in a fight for a pennant, and this was a team thing and the last thing in my mind was the Triple Crown. At that time the focus of attention wasn't on me, it was on the team. The important thing was winning the pennant, and my idea was to just go out and try to help the team win. Nothing else mattered.

That was the climax of the season, that three-game series at Kansas City. Up to then I had done nothing in Kansas City. I hadn't hit any home runs there. As a matter of fact, I hadn't even come close. Their young pitching had done a job on me.

But I caught on in this series.

We won the first game 4–0, with a rookie, Tom Phoebus, who had been recently recalled from our Rochester farm team, pitching his second straight shutout. And I finally hit a home run in the ball park, my forty-seventh of the season. I also doubled and drove in two of our four runs.

In the second game, it looked like we were out of it. Kansas City led 6–1 through six. But in the top of the seventh I hit a two-run home run. And in the eighth we got seven runs (I hit another in that inning) and we pulled it out, 10–8.

The third game, on September 22, was our biggest game of the season. We beat Kansas City 6–1. I had two doubles and a single (one of the hits missing by a foot from being my fiftieth home run) and drove in two runs. That gave me eight runs batted in for the series and clinched the RBI leg of the Triple Crown. Oh, yes, with that victory, we also clinched the American League pennant.

Oh, what a celebration. I thought the one I went through in Cincinnati in 1961 was something, but this one was too much. We were in that clubhouse for about three hours with beer and champagne and mustard and cake and mayonnaise and sliced tomatoes splashing over everybody. Somebody smacked me in the mouth with a piece of cake and I stuffed a rubber snake in Luis Aparicio's shoe. Louie was so jumpy he almost went through the ceiling when he saw that. He let out a scream and kicked the shoe across the clubhouse.

Chocolate milk was streaming down the front of Baltimore writer Gordon Beard's undershirt. I ran over and placed my arm next to the milk stain for comparison. "Now you know how I feel," I said. "See how you like it."

Then they smeared me with shaving cream from my nose to the chin. What could I do? I spread out my arms like Al Jolson and sang, "Mammy."

Nobody in that clubhouse was thinking of the future—the World Series coming up—or the past. It was the present, only the present that counted. We were so happy and pleased because we had gone so far as a team. Gone as far as you can go in this game of baseball. It was one of the happiest moments of our lives and we were trying to hold onto it as long as we could.

And Boog Powell snuck up behind me with a loaded champagne bottle and poured the stuff down the back of my neck.

"Booger," I cried, "stop that! You know I can't swim."

But old Crisco didn't stop, and I didn't care. The party was just starting.

17 Three Lifetime Thrills—
in Four Games

I hit my forty-ninth home run of the 1966 season on September 21. I spent the next eight games trying, without success, to hit home run no. 50. I also spent some of the time thinking about the World Series.

I had been hoping since 1961 to get back into a World Series. That was the year Cincinnati lost to the Yankees in five games—and my performance had been just terrible. The team was depending on my hitting and I batted .200 and I felt I had let everyone down. Naturally, a player always wants to get into as many World Series as he can. But my feeling was, I wanted to make one more Series and try, this time, to get on the winning side.

Looking at the three teams fighting for the National League pennant—the Dodgers, Pirates, and Giants—there was no question in my mind that we would have the best chance against the Dodgers. When I told that to the press, some of the reporters laughed at me. "The Dodgers?" they said. "Face that great pitching staff? You must be crazy. You must be out of your mind wanting to play them."

I was never more clearheaded.

The Pirates and Giants were built like us. They were hitting teams. We knew what our hitters could do to their clubs, but what would the Pirate and Giant hitters do to us? The Dodgers were different. Their attack consisted of single, single, walk, stolen base, sacrifice fly, and trying to capitalize on the other fellow's mistakes. Like Sandy Koufax wrote in his autobiography: "Our game was the bunt, the steal and the sacrifice. . . . Someone would beat out a hit, be sacrificed to second, steal third, and score on the overthrow. Then we would gather the wagons into a circle around the dugout."

I felt our ball club could handle that kind of a team. We had a good defense and I was sure we could score some runs against Koufax, Drysdale, or whomever they sent out there. If we could get five or six innings out of our young starters, our real fine bullpen would be ready to work. I felt that our pitchers could hold the Dodgers to three or four runs, which meant that we would be in the ball game all the way. Then, with one or two swings of the bat, we could break it up.

It was nice to know, too, that if we played the Dodgers, we would come out of the Series ahead on the money side. Dodger Stadium holds more people than either Candlestick Park in San Francisco or Forbes Field in Pittsburgh, and the Dodgers have more box seats than any ball club in the National League. As it turned out, we got $11,600 per man playing the Dodgers. If we had played San Francisco or Pittsburgh, we would have gotten three or four thousand dollars less.

There was another factor, too, in my preference for the Dodgers. When I was with Cincinnati the Dodgers always were our chief rivals. The press talked about feuds between the Dodgers and Reds, and it was true. There had been some fights and bad words between us. It seemed they were always blocking the way when we were going after a pennant. We hated them and they hated us.

Then I would be facing my old friend, Don Drysdale. As I have indicated, over the years he has griped me more than any other opponent. Between trying to figure out a way to hit him, and picking myself up from the dirt— especially those times when I knew he was throwing at me deliberately—he really got to me. It wasn't just that he was knocking me down. It was that he was also getting me out. I just wasn't able to figure out a way to hit him. And that's what really bothered me, not the part where he was knocking me down all the time.

I don't mean to excuse Drysdale or any other pitcher who deliberately throws at a hitter. I don't think that any pitcher belongs on the mound if he feels he has to throw at a hitter to try to get him out. It is a very dangerous thing to purposely throw at a hitter. Hitters have been killed that way and some have been maimed for life.

The pitcher's excuse always seems to be, "The batter's taking the bread out of my mouth." Well, where does that leave the hitter who is consistently being retired by the pitcher? I mean, you don't see a hitter throwing a bat at a pitcher, do you (not too often, anyway)? The hitter just has to battle his way the best he can, and it should be the same way with the pitcher. If he can't get a hitter out with his natural stuff, he should try to figure out some other way to pitch him. I don't think a pitcher should ever feel he has to throw at a hitter deliberately to get him out.

So Don Drysdale was one Dodger I knew very well, and one thing I knew about Don Drysdale in 1966 was that he had slipped as a pitcher.

In the last two or three years, Don had moved from side-arm to about three-quarters. I don't know how this came about, but I do know they had been trying to get him up on top a little bit, from directly sidearm to about three-quarters overhand. I think it may have been more for control of his curve ball. But whatever it was, his ball didn't run in on you as much, he had lost a little of that zip off his fast ball and he'd become more of a spot pitcher, trying more or less to pitch to spots rather than just letting the ball go with his natural movement to take care of the hitters. Now he wasn't as overpowering against right-handed hitters, and in my last two or three years in the National League I hit him much better. And I told my teammates this, and it was one of the reasons why we liked our chances against the Dodgers.

There wasn't much I could add to the scouting report on

the Dodgers. Jim Russo, our chief scout, and his staff, had prepared a real good one. The day before the Series started we worked out at Dodger Stadium and after the workouts they handed out the scouting report.

We spent about 2½ hours going over the report. We took the Dodger players individually and went over their strong points and weaknesses offensively and defensively. With the pitchers, the report told what each pitcher would probably rely on more in certain situations, how good his fast ball was, how good his control was, how good his breaking ball was, and the percentage of times they would throw the fast ball and the curve ball . . . things like that.

Here and there, I would add a little bit, based on my own experiences of playing against these fellows over a period of years. For instance, in the scouting reports on Ron Perranoski, they said he threw a curve ball, fast ball, change-up. They left out the slider. But Perranoski does have a slider and I alerted them to it.

On Jim Gilliam the report was that he didn't have too much power and couldn't handle the real good fast ball any more. "Just don't walk him," it said. But I said, "Look, if Gilliam gets ahead of a pitcher, say a count of 3–1, or a count of 2–0, in that situation where he can look for a fast ball, he can hit it with good power."

We got to kidding around a bit. The scouts came back and said, "Robby, we've seen him hit the ball, and he didn't show us too much power."

I said, "Gentlemen, I've seen him for ten years. I've seen him get the pitcher in a hole, 3–1, and look for the fast ball, and really hit it good, hit a few home runs in fact." So they added that tidbit to the CIA file on Jim Gilliam.

There were other things, too. I said to our catcher, Andy Etchebarren, "Andy, when that Wills gets on base, he's almost always going to go on the first or second pitch." That wasn't in the scouting reports. And I also had some advice for our shortstop and second baseman. I told them to be very careful when Johnny Roseboro or Lou Johnson came into second base because those two fellows came in hard and were real tough sliders. The other Dodger players didn't come in quite as hard as they do. Roseboro and Johnson come in to break up the play, to take you out of the play. I told them to be very alert when they came in there.

Aside from that, some of the players had questions of their own. Curt Blefary came up to me and said, "When I'm out there in left field I'm gonna watch you on every hitter. I want you to help me out, move me around if you think I'm in the wrong place. If you think I'm in the right place, just let me know."

And that's what happened. Blefary watched me on every hitter and I'd move him in and out, back or over in the outfield. Paul Blair in center field watched me a little bit. The second baseman, Davey Johnson, would turn around once in a while and I would move him a little bit here and there. It all came out of my own knowledge of the Dodgers after playing against most of them for so many years.

Naturally, everyone wanted to know about Sandy Koufax, especially the young ballplayers. Was he as great as they had heard? I assured them, one and all, that he was even better than they had heard. I said, "You have to bear down against him at all times, put out that little bit of extra effort because that's what he's doing all the time, and he's such an outstanding performer that even when he doesn't have his real stuff, he can still get by and pitch a great ball game."

I told them that Koufax never sidearms anyone, that his ball doesn't move in or out. It goes up, it takes off, and the thing about him is that you have to try and lay off the high fast ball. That's what quite a number of hitters didn't do. They were just so anxious to get out in front of his fast ball and they were so wound up, that they'd swing at a lot of bad balls. The ball is up so you can see it all the way and you just want to jump on it so badly that you swing at it. That's a tough pitch to hit, especially against a Koufax who's got a little extra, and the ball takes off when it's up that high.

I told them too that Sandy had a real good curve ball. I said he had struggled along with it during the season but I told them not to even think about that. "Just remember," I said, "he does have a good overhand curve ball and he throws from the same spot all the time. He never varies his pitching motion and he very seldom throws to first base with a man on first. He has a bad move to first base and he just doesn't hold the man on base real close. Just go up there and bear down," I said, "and if you get a strike off this guy, take your cuts."

We got a real break when Sandy had to pitch on the last day of the season. We never expected it. The Dodgers needed a victory in the first game of their doubleheader with the Phillies, or a Giant loss against Pittsburgh, otherwise Koufax would have to pitch the second game. That's what happened. The Giants beat Pittsburgh and stayed alive, and the Phillies won the first game of the doubleheader, and so Sandy had to pitch the second game and win for the Dodgers to clinch the pennant. Sandy won and we knew that manager Walt Alston probably wouldn't start Koufax on the first day of the Series with only two days' rest. If he did start he probably wouldn't be as effective as he would with three or four days' rest. We were just keeping our fingers crossed, and I think the key to the Series was Koufax not being able to start the first game.

I talked with Sandy on the morning of the first game. He came over and we shook hands and he congratulated me on my year and he said, "You really went over there and showed them what you could do."

Then a photographer came over and posed us and I said to Sandy, "If I pose with you you're going to have to throw me all change-ups when you pitch."

But it was Don Drysdale who was going to pitch the first game for the Dodgers, and I was ready for him.

I went in that ball game free and easy, and so did my teammates, and that's what really surprised me. At least I had played in a World Series before, but only a couple of them had. And don't let anyone tell you differently—there is no pressure to compare with World Series pressure.

Sure, I have heard players say that the World Series is the icing on the cake, that winning the pennant is the main thing. Sandy Koufax wrote in his book that to him the pressure of the pennant race was much more intense than the pressure of the World Series. Not to me. A pennant race could start in June, could start in July, even in May, and go on right down to the last day of the season. But you've got sixty, seventy, eighty games to play in a tight pennant race and you know there's always a tomorrow, at least until you get down to the last day of the season. But in the World Series you know it's the best four out of seven and each game is *the* game, the big game, and there's no getting 'em tomorrow because there is no tomorrow. Each game you lose is a game that cuts your chances shorter and shorter. You just feel you must win each game.

That's pressure. Then comes the added pressure in knowing that millions of people are watching you. The stands are filled and you're being watched on television all over the country—by your family, your friends, and people who haven't seen you play ball before. All eyes are on you and you want to perform well in front of these people, in front of them all. And you want to do something you'll always remember and that you'll always be remembered for.

With all of that, the fellows went out as if it were just another ball game. There was no rah-rah, no one to go around and try to break the tension, because there was no tension. The relaxed feeling was there. We were confident. We knew we had a real good ball club, that we had overcome a lot of things to win the American League pennant. We kept reading in the papers that we didn't belong on the same ball field with the Dodgers, that we came from a Mickey Mouse league and things like that. And maybe that helped us, too. We just felt that we were going to beat the Dodgers, and that's the way we took the field at Los Angeles to open the 1966 World Series.

So when I got ready to bat against Drysdale I was real loose. It wasn't like the 1961 World Series batting against Whitey Ford and just not being able to figure out a way to hit him. I felt I had matured as a hitter since then. I was a little smarter at the plate. I knew now what the pitchers were trying to do in certain situations and what they weren't going to do and what I was going to do and what I was going to look for. Now I was a little better hitter and a little more mature, not only as a ballplayer, but as a person.

Drysdale got the first batter, Luis Aparicio, then he walked Russ Snyder. Now I knew Drysdale would try to come inside on me to try to hit me on the fists—especially with a man on base and on the first pitch because I do hit the first pitch quite often. Don has an interesting pitch that is called a sinker but isn't really a sinker. It's actually a spitter. And I knew he might try that on the first pitch, come inside on me with the sinker, which breaks down, and go for the double play. He did throw this sinker, which isn't a sinker but which is called a sinker. It was down low and I laid off and that made the count one ball and no strikes.

At the risk of losing my good standing in the Batter's League of America, I would like to make a suggestion here and now. And that is that they legalize the spitball.

As it is today, the hitter is just caught in a twilight world. I think it's a terrible mental strain on a hitter to know the pitcher is throwing the spitter and nothing can be done about it. If it was a legal pitch at least you could look for it, or know the pitcher might throw it, and you wouldn't worry quite as much about it. You'd just go up there and do the best you could against the pitcher who was throwing it, and I think you would come out better against it.

Now all you can do is keep calling for the ball. The umpires check it and won't see anything and throw it back and all the pitcher has to do is get a little bit more on his fingers and there he goes. He throws the pitch and the bottom drops out of it and you know it's a spitter and you know the umpire recognizes it, but he just can't enforce it. I think the way things are going now it would be better to legalize the pitch, because now the batter is halfway and in-between, with no place to go.

So that was Drysdale's first pitch to me, and now I was looking for the fast ball inside. I felt that he would come in on me, hit me on the fists, try to get me to hit into a double play that way. And he did come inside with the fast ball and I was looking for it and I was ready.

A lot of people looked at me like I was a little off when I told them afterwards that I got jammed on that pitch. When I say I got jammed I meant I hit the ball down toward the trademark and I really didn't know whether I had hit it well enough to make the stands. I was watching it quite anxiously. I knew I had a good shot because I had hit it in the right direction, almost down the line, and that's only 340 feet, and I knew I had a chance if it was far enough back where the outfielder couldn't reach into the stands for it.

I don't think I reached first base when I saw it fall in. Then everything went blank. I think I floated around the bases. I don't remember a thing until I got back to the dugout.

In the pounding and noise and congratulations that followed, all I remember is one precious remark from one of my teammates. I don't know who it was, but one of the fellows came up to me and said, loud enough for all to hear, "Robby, I knew you would hit no. 50 sooner or later."

Then I sat down and watched Brooks follow me with a home run and I felt great. I was back down to earth by then and it was just wonderful because now we had a 3–0 lead right there in the first inning and I felt that might almost be enough to win, although you never feel you have enough runs.

But we had done just what we wanted to do against the Dodgers; get out in front of them and take away their running game.

Then Dave McNally went out and had control trouble. He walked three straight men in the third and I was standing out in right field thinking, this is the way this ball club beats you, on your mistakes. You walk them and they'll throw in a base hit, steal a base, and they're off and running. And that's all I kept thinking—here we go, this is what we didn't want to do. This is what we wanted to avoid and we're right in the middle of it right now. I was just hoping Dave would throw strikes. But he wasn't able to on this day.

So Moe Drabowsky came in and became a hero and a lot of people wanted to know where this guy had been all year. Well, he had done a tremendous job for us all year long. He was 6–0 on the season and he had come in many times and cut the ball club off. The only thing that surprised me about his performance against the Dodgers was his eleven strike-outs in his 6⅔ innings (a World Series record for relief pitchers).

After he walked the one man, Gilliam, Moe just threw strikes. He moved the ball around and out and mixed his pitches and the Dodgers were too far behind (it was 5–2 now) to play their game. They had to hit their way on and Moe wouldn't let them because he was throwing strikes and just doing a tremendous job.

Now we had three to go and if we could beat Sandy Koufax in Los Angeles we'd really have the firepower when we returned home. My plan of attack against Koufax was simple: Always try to hit his fast ball and not let him get to the curve ball because he has an outstanding curve. With Koufax you just go up there looking for the fast ball. Make sure it's a good strike—you have to lay off the high fast ball—and get the bat out in front.

Sandy was just about as good as we knew he would be in the first three or four innings. He had his good fast ball and he was getting the curve ball over and we couldn't get to him. Meanwhile, I almost messed things up for our side.

In the second inning Lou Johnson broke his bat and hit a ball to short right field, toward the line. I was shading toward right-center and had a long way to come for the ball. When I was almost to it I knew I had to come fast because the Dodgers like to take the extra base, especially a player like Johnson who is running hard from the time he leaves home plate and is looking for that extra base.

Just as I got to the ball I could see Johnson rounding first and still digging. I fielded the ball barehanded and when I went to turn to throw to second, my bad knee gave out on me. And I went down. I got up and threw the ball in but he was in at second easily. We managed to get out of that inning, but Hank Bauer had no gold star for me when I returned to the dugout.

In the fourth inning Koufax walked me and then Brooks hit a slow ground ball toward short. Jim Gilliam went over toward the hole to try and field the ball and it went off his glove. He and Wills started after the ball at the same time and no one was covering third, so I broke. But as I started toward third, Wills was back to the base. I tried to stop and the knee gave out again. I couldn't get back to second base and I was an easy out. It was a little embarrassing at the time but all was forgotten after what happened in the fifth inning.

We got three runs in the fifth because Willie Davis committed three errors. Go figure that. Actually, what happened to Davis could have happened to anyone. But you just don't expect it to happen to a fellow who is as good a fielder as Davis. After that it just wasn't the same for Sandy. It looked like he was reaching back to get a little extra to strike out the hitters. He seemed to be a little tired and he didn't have the real zip on his fast ball and he wasn't as smooth as the Koufax you're used to watching out there on the mound.

In the sixth inning he got another tough break when I hit a triple that should have been caught. It was a drive between center and right and either Willie Davis or Ron Fairly could have taken the ball easily. But neither man called for it. I think that Davis was looking for a little help after his three errors, that he was hoping Fairly would catch the ball. But I can understand Fairly, because the way the Dodgers play their outfield, the left fielder and right fielder don't shade toward center field too much. They more or less play toward the line. Davis, with his tremendous speed, can cover so much ground that they let him take just about everything he can get to. I'm sure that Fairly felt that Willie was going to catch the ball. So he pulled up. In the picture taken of the play you can see both of them pulling up at the same time and the ball going between them.

Boog Powell singled me home and that was the ball game. We won 6–0 and Jim Palmer pitched a tremendous game, allowing the Dodgers only four hits. And we went back home in a great frame of mind. Originally, most of us felt it would be a hard, tough Series, that it would go six or seven games. But after we won that second ball game in Los Angeles, we felt like a new ball club. We felt now we could win it in four straight.

We got fantastic pitching again in the third game. Wally Bunker pitched a six-hitter and held the Dodgers scoreless and Paul Blair hit a fifth-inning home run off Claude Osteen and that was it, 1–0.

Now it was Don Drysdale again and this time he pitched a remarkable game, and I just got a little lucky with him in the fourth inning.

It was scoreless going to the bottom of the fourth and Russ Snyder led off by hitting the first pitch for an out. Just before I left the on-deck circle I almost talked myself into taking Drysdale's first pitch. My reasoning was that if I hit the first pitch and made an out, Drysdale would have two outs on two pitches. Then Brooks would be coming up behind me and he would have to take a pitch. He would be forced to take a pitch. Usually the manager doesn't like to see an enemy pitcher get out of what he calls an easy inning on three pitches. So if the first two batters have gone out on two pitches, he'll tell the third batter to take the pitch. It's almost an unwritten rule that one of the three hitters has to take one pitch at least. And usually it's the middle man because you don't really want to force the guy behind you to take a pitch.

So I almost talked myself into it. Then as I settled into the batter's box, I changed my mind. I always talk to myself at bat and this time the monologue went like this: I'll look for a certain pitch, a good pitch. If it's a good pitch, I'll take a real good swing at it. And if I make out, well at least I got a good pitch to hit. And maybe I can get one I can hit real good.

And that's what happened. Drysdale threw me a fast ball right down the middle of the plate, belt high. That really surprised me but I got good wood on it and as soon as I hit it I knew it was gone. I think Drysdale knew it too, because as soon as it connected he dropped his head and kicked the dirt. He didn't even turn around to look at the flight of the ball.

The best description I've ever read of me running the bases on a home run came after that game from Jimmy Cannon. He wrote that I "suggested a man who leans against a wind with sleet in it, the head down to keep the stones out of his eyes."

Not stones, Jimmy. Stardust. I loped around those bases thinking that the day before Paul Blair had hit one in the fifth inning and it stood up, and this was the fourth inning. I was thinking, well, I hope this stands up. I hope this is enough to win this ball game.

And it was. Thanks to Dave McNally's brilliant pitching, that run did hold up, and we had won the World Series in four straight. And that, you might say, was my third lifetime thrill in four games.

My first-game home run and my fourth-game home run

were the two biggest thrills of my lifetime. Before I hit those I always looked back to my first base hit in the major leagues in my first at-bat, playing on a pennant winner in 1961, hitting a home run in the 1961 World Series. Those all meant a lot to me personally, but not as much as the homers in 1966.

But the biggest thrill of all—bigger even than those home runs—was beating the Dodgers the way we did. A lot of people have since tried to excuse the Dodger performance. They said they were tired. I can't buy that at all. They knew, just like us, that they were playing for eleven or twelve thousand dollars. You don't go out and throw that kind of money down the drain. The Dodgers, I felt, played as well as they could. It was unfortunate that Wills was hampered with a bad leg which slowed his running game, and that some of the other Dodgers were in a little slump. But I can't buy the idea that they were a tired ball club, that they had been in a tough pennant race and it had taken a lot out of them. The Dodgers are always in tough pennant races. In 1965 they were in a tough fight to win the pennant and they went on to beat Minnesota in seven games.

What it was, I think, was that we were the hungry ball club and they weren't. I had the feeling that we wanted to win a little more. Maybe they took us too lightly. Maybe they felt that all they had to do to beat us was come out on the field and we would run and hide from them, which we didn't do. We didn't wait for them to come to us. We took the game to them.

And there was never any doubt in my mind that we would beat them. I think it just proves that, if you're dedicated to a cause, if you want something badly enough, you can really do it. That was our ball club in 1966, and that was our ball club in the World Series.

18   *After the Slide*

I spend six weeks in June and July of 1967 babying my busted
head, waiting for my vision to clear. And, while I'm waiting,
the Orioles lose seventeen of twenty-eight games and sink
lower into the American League. And this isn't the way it
is supposed to be at all.

But, then, nothing is really what it seems.

I came out of the 1966 season with the idea that I might
just possibly be able to capitalize on my temporary fame by
making a certain amount of extra money from endorsements
and personal appearances—things like that. But I put a very
realistic figure on it. Being a *Negro* Triple Crown winner was,
I knew, not going to make me rich. I thought I might earn
between twenty and thirty thousand dollars in the off-season.
I thought it was a very low figure and I said, well, let's see if
I make that, or do better than that.

I made less than ten thousand.

Not one endorsement came my way. I did make twenty
to twenty-five personal appearances, but the majority were
for expenses only.

So that brought me down to earth very quick.

Then we had trouble renting a house in Baltimore and
that bumped me a little more.

We had had some trouble my first year in Baltimore.
The club did find us a house to rent but when my wife saw it
she was appalled. It was dirty and run-down and she felt it
was unfit for the kids. So we all had to spend a week in a
hotel before we found a house that was right for us.

Then a real-estate broker who had heard about our troubles

came to us. "Don't worry about it," he said. "Next year you won't have any trouble."

I said, "Fine, but you'll find it isn't that easy."

He said, "Tell me what you want—air conditioning, fenced-in yard, etc."

I told him that all I wanted was a suitable house. I didn't care if it was in a segregated or integrated neighborhood. I wanted the kind of place I could bring my wife and kids. It was that simple. No problem, he said.

But there was a problem and, through the winter, he still hadn't found us a house. Finally, I got anxious and started calling him and it was always . . . "no, but I'm working on it."

Then, a week before the start of spring training, he called. He said, "I've got a perfect house for you—three bedrooms." He described it and I said, "That's great. Take it."

He called back the next day. "The lady says she doesn't want to rent it."

"Why?"

"She changed her mind."

"Why?" I repeated, "just because she doesn't want to rent it to a Negro?"

"No, it's not her. Her father-in-law doesn't want her to. He's afraid what the neighbors might say."

I sighed, "I told you it wouldn't be easy."

I was upset. I called Harry Dalton, the Orioles' business manager, and explained the situation to him. I said, "I'm coming to spring training to get myself in condition, but when we break camp and I still don't have a house that's suitable for us, I'm going home. I'm not going to put my family through what they went through last year. If I don't have a house for my family I'm not going to come up to play baseball."

Mr. Hoffberger called back and told me not to worry, that he'd get something. The club was very good about it throughout, but the problem was still there.

Finally, my real estate man called me again and said the woman had changed her mind, she would give us the house.

"How come?" I asked.

"Well, I went to her neighbors and they said they would be delighted and proud to have Frank Robinson as a neighbor."

So that's how Frank Robinson, the ballplayer, got a house for his family. If I was Frank Robinson, just plain Negro, I'd probably still be looking.

But I must say I was received very well in Baltimore, from the time I first joined the club. Once we got settled my family was accepted like anyone else and treated just fine. Our neighbors were very considerate and that made it much easier to perform my duties out on the field, because I knew my family was all right and they were happy. I wasn't subject to outside pressures and I was able to concentrate fully on baseball. I was, and am, very pleased and happy with Baltimore—the city and the team.

Of course I would have been a lot happier about the team if we could have done a little better in 1967. The way the season in the American League turned out—with four inferior teams fighting for a pennant—I felt we might have won the pennant easier than we had in 1966, *if* we had played anywhere up to our 1966 form. But as early as June of '67, when I got into that controversy over the newspaper interview in which I said that the club wasn't playing up to its potential —even at that time I could see that we weren't going anywhere.

Looking back, I think the worst thing that could have happened to us was when we won our first three games of the season. We beat Minnesota twice, then Kansas City. And, right away, a lot of players felt . . . here we go again, we'll win this thing again.

Even two months into the season, when we were maybe three or four games out of first, some of the guys would say, "All we need is a four- or five-game winning streak and we'll be all right." But we never could win four in a row, not until the last month of the season when it didn't matter any more.

Exactly what I was trying to point out in that June interview came to pass. We didn't change our attitudes, we didn't get to be more aggressive. We just seemed to think that because we were the champs, all we had to do was go out on the field and we'd win.

I was possibly more aware of what was going on because I had been through the same kind of thing with the Cincinnati Reds in 1964 and '65, 1965 especially. We were picked to win that year and we never won more than four games in a row and whenever we needed a ball game to put us over the top something would happen and we'd lose it.

That was the way it was in '67, plus our whole team just seemed to go bad. We lost all of our 1966 starting pitchers with bad arms—Steve Barber, Wally Bunker, Jim Palmer, and finally Dave McNally. Our bullpen wasn't as dependable as it had been, plus Brooks Robinson had a bad first half and Boog Powell had a complete off-season. And we just didn't play well. We beat ourselves at bat, we made too many errors, we just couldn't make the big play. It was a combination of a lot of things and I just hope we got it all out of our systems.

For I really believe we do have a sound ball club and that we can become genuine contenders again in 1968, and the future.

I think, too, that I should certainly be able to help the ball club the way I didn't help them in 1967. The Orioles lost seventeen of twenty-eight games while I was recovering from the double-blinks, and I like to think that we might have won a few more games if I had been sound. At the time that it happened I was leading the league with a .337 average, I was leading in home runs with twenty-one, and I had fifty-nine runs batted in. I figured then that I had a good shot at repeating as Triple Crown winner, which is something no one in the history of baseball has ever done. I really did feel that way, though I know I could have hit a slump and, as it turned out, would have had a very difficult time trying to beat out Carl Yastrzemski, who just had a tremendous year. But I would have been right up there, I know that.

Instead, I sat around and waited for the eyes to refocus, and while I waited, I did some thinking. I thought, well, I'm thirty-two years old now, I better start figuring out what I'm going to do after my playing days. And the one thought came to me: that some day soon, major league baseball is going to have its first Negro manager; and, though I don't expect that I'll be first, I would very much like to manage in the major leagues some day.

I know one thing. I'm ready right now to manage. And if someone called me today and offered me a good contract, I would have to sit down and think about it, talk to my wife about it, and really seriously consider giving up my playing career.

The reason I doubt strongly that I'll be major league baseball's first Negro manager is that I'm with the wrong ball club. What I mean is that there are now three clubs in baseball that are prime clubs for Negro managers—the Dodgers, Giants, and Chicago Cubs. Each of these teams is owned by old-line owners, each is playing in an area where acceptance would come readily. Horace Stoneham, the owner of the Giants, has been close to Willie Mays ever since Willie came up, and I think Willie Mays could manage right now. He would be a good choice, a very popular choice. I don't know if he would accept it or not—I don't know if he's that type. But I believe he could make a fine manager.

There have been a number of outstanding Negro players on the Dodgers and Walter O'Malley's only problem would be finding the right one. The leading candidates, I imagine, would be Jim Gilliam and John Roseboro who is now with the Twins. And Phil Wrigley at Chicago has Ernie Banks, Mr. Cub. I think Banks would make an excellent manager.

Another thing about all the owners I mentioned—Stoneham, O'Malley, and Wrigley: all are independent owners, they don't have to answer to anyone, they've been in the game a long, long time and they could make such a move without creating a big furor.

But the hiring of a Negro manager is not going to come out of a clear blue sky. It's not going to come tomorrow or the day after. I mean, some clubowner might just get that bold and reach down and pluck a Negro who is in baseball now, in the middle of his career, and make him manager. But I doubt it.

I think it's going to have to come gradually. There are barely any Negroes now in a non-playing capacity in professional baseball. There are a couple of coaches, a handful of scouts, and that's it. You can't tell me that of all the Negroes who have been in baseball, even those who never played major league ball, that some aren't qualified to make good front-office men. It's the same old story, the owners are just afraid, are a step behind the public. Once one owner breaks the line, I'm sure the others will follow.

I think Bill Russell in basketball, the coach of the Boston Celtics, has proven that a Negro can do the job, and can be respected by the fans, and by his players. I don't think any true baseball fan would look at me as a Negro *or* white man if my team—the team I'm managing, the team he's rooting for—is winning. And if the team is losing, you're a bum anyway, black or white.

But the people who run baseball have to catch up to the public. It's a little better for the Negro now when he gets out of baseball. In the old days he couldn't find any jobs. Now he can get into public relations work with big companies and things like that. But most of them still aren't able to stay in baseball—in the front office, as a coach, as a scout or anything. They aren't able to hook on. White ballplayers when they retire are made pitching coaches, they are made hitting coaches, they are made bullpen coaches, they are made scouts, they get jobs in the minors—they get to stay in baseball. But it hasn't happened to Negroes. Very qualified fellows like George Crowe, Larry Doby, and Monte Irvin have applied for jobs in baseball and been turned down. When Brooks Lawrence finally retired from baseball, the Reds made him a part-time scout in the Ohio area. But I don't think he had any real authority to sign anyone. And the next year, they dropped him. I know that in the last couple of years he has applied for a job with the Cincinnati ball club and they've refused him. But they always seem to find some kind of spot for the white guy. Naturally, they can't find a spot for everybody, but one Negro, two Negroes? Is that going to tear down the power structure?

Yet I still think this is going to change and I hope I'll be part of the change. I can see change taking place off the field. When I first came up with the Cincinnati ball club there were quite a few fellows from the southern states on the club. I never had any trouble with them on the field or anyplace else, really, but we just never socialized off the field. That's changing now. Now you will find that fellows are inviting each other to their homes for dinner and are going out together to movies and theaters and things like that. And they do it naturally because they just get along with each other. The thinking today is different. I think prejudice and discrimination is slowly, slowly being pushed out of baseball, that each individual is being judged more and more on what he is able to do as a man, as an individual; he is no longer being judged by the color of his skin.

It *is* a gradual process though. In George Plimpton's book, *Paper Lion*, a white player, John Gordy of the Detroit Lions, summed up the situation very well, I thought. He said: "You come to this league with your prejudices already set for you—from your home, your school—and not much happens to change them. What is increased is understanding. After all, you're living together, playing together, and you learn it's easy enough. Perhaps that undermines the prejudice. But not too much. We get along."

We *do* get along and it's going to get better and I hope I'll be part of that better day, especially when the breakthrough comes in baseball off the playing field.

I've thought often about managing—the pitfalls, the rewards, whether I really can do the job. I've kept mental notes on all the managers I played under, their strengths, their weaknesses. And I've played under a series of fine managers, from Birdie Tebbetts to Hank Bauer. They were all different types of managers, and I've learned from them all. That doesn't mean I'd necessarily become a Birdie Tebbetts type or a Hank Bauer type or a combination Tebbetts-Hutchinson-Bauer manager. I would try to apply all the knowledge gathered from these baseball men and try to use it my own unique way. But always I would have to be my own man.

On July 29, I go back into the lineup. The Indians' starting pitcher is John O'Donoghue, a left-hander, and I think I can see the ball better if the pitcher is a left-hander. So I tell Hank I want to play and he says okay and puts me in left field, which is a little easier to play than right field.

It works all right that day. I look at a called strike in the first inning, bounce out to the first baseman in the second, single past the shortstop into center field in the fifth, strike out in the seventh, and walk in the ninth. One-for-four, and it's okay. In the field I catch seven fly balls. The ball comes out to me sort of the way it does when you're running on your heels—sort of bobbing up and down. But I can see well enough.

And I start playing regularly and, that first month back, it is not that okay. In fact it is frightening and I kind of luck through it. It is frightening up there hitting because I simply cannot pick up the ball. And lots of times I ask myself: Am I being fair to the team? Could someone else be doing a better job?

I have to adjust my hitting and, consequently, I get into a lot of bad habits. I begin pulling away from the ball and committing myself before really knowing what the pitch is. I am hitting off my front foot, shifting my weight to my back foot. I can't check my swing like I could. Once I make up my mind I have to go on and swing. And I have to make up my mind fast. I am scared to take a pitch. I can't tell whether it's a ball or a strike. So I stand up at the plate frightened, like it was in 1958 after Camilo Pascual hit me in the head. I stand up there, not able to see the pitch properly, not knowing whether I'll be hit in the face or hit in the head or be injured permanently.

But after that month, my vision improves considerably. It never does come back 100 percent, right up to the very end of the '67 season. I still have trouble judging the speed of the ball and the spin on the ball, but I get through all right. And, under the circumstances, I guess it's not as bad a year as it might have been. I end up batting .311, second only to Carl Yastrzemski in the American League, with ninety-four runs batted in and thirty home runs.

And there are a couple of highlights. My twenty-seventh home run of the season is the four-hundredth of my career. Only Mickey Mantle, and Ed Mathews of the active players in our league have hit that many. I hit it off a good pitcher, too, Jim Kaat of the Twins, a fast ball that goes 380 or 390 feet.

Then, in the last week of the season, batting against José Santiago of the Red Sox, I lead off in the sixth inning and I hit one past shortstop in the hole. And that one is my two-thousandth hit. Only nine other active players have gotten that many hits, but no one knows I have done it. When I get to first base I tell umpire Bill Kinnamon, "I'd like to have that ball—that's no. 2000."

He doesn't even hear me. "What?" he mutters.

I say, "I'd like to have that ball—that's no. 2000."

He is startled. "Oh, congratulations," and he gets the ball for me.

In truth, neither milestone means as much to me anyway,

because of the way the season turns out, but when I'm out of this game, when it's all over with me as a player, that's when the meaning will deepen.

What kind of a thought is that, anyway? Now the pursuit is for five hundred home runs and three thousand hits. I'll be thirty-three years old on my next birthday and I think I have three or four good years left in me. I hope I do because I want to play this game as long as I can play it well. When I can't play it well any longer, I'll get out. Every old-timer says that, I know, but I like to think I really will get out.

I'll get out with regrets, of course, but no regrets over the past. I've been criticized lots of times for what I did or what I said off the field. But I don't regret anything I said, anything I did. I never tried to hurt anyone and I always tried to do my best. I have a clear conscience.

To go out there and give 100 percent is all you can do. I give the best I can, and that's the truth.

The month I played with the double-blinks, the month I played in fear because I couldn't tell if the ball coming at me at seventy or eighty miles an hour was a curve ball or a fast ball, my wife said to me, "Frank, why can't you take it easy, why don't you look out for yourself?"

I said, "I can't play that way." And that's the truth, too, the one truth I know about this game and about myself.

FRANK ROBINSON'S MINOR LEAGUE AND MAJOR LEAGUE RECORD

Year	Club	G	AB	R	H	2B	3B	HR	RBI	BB	SO	AVE.
1953	Ogden	72	270	70	94	20	6	17	83	53	69	.348
1954	Tulsa	8	30	4	8	0	0	0	1	. .	. .	.267
1954	Columbia	132	491	*112	165	32	9	25	110	88	65	.336
1955	Columbia	80	243	50	64	15	7	12	52	41	44	.263
1956	Cincinnati	152	572	*122	166	27	6	38	83	64	95	.290
1957	Cincinnati	150	611	97	197	29	5	29	75	44	92	.322
1958	Cincinnati	148	554	90	149	25	6	31	83	62	80	.269
1959	Cincinnati	146	540	106	168	31	4	36	125	69	93	.311
1960	Cincinnati	139	464	86	138	33	6	31	83	82	67	.297
1961	Cincinnati	153	545	117	176	32	7	37	124	71	64	.323
1962	Cincinnati	162	609	*134	208	*51	2	39	136	76	62	.342
1963	Cincinnati	140	482	79	125	19	3	21	91	81	69	.259
1964	Cincinnati	156	568	103	174	38	6	29	96	79	67	.306
1965	Cincinnati	156	582	109	172	33	5	33	113	70	18	.296
1966	Baltimore	155	576	*122	182	34	2	*49	*122	87	90	*.316
1967	Baltimore	129	479	83	149	23	7	30	94	71	84	.311
Major League Totals		1786	6582	1248	2004	375	59	403	1225	856	963	.304

* Led League